The Lord's Supper Pattern Book:
Imagining Harriet Powers' Lost Bible Story Quilt

By Kyra E. Hicks

Black Threads Press
Arlington, Virginia

© 2011 Kyra E. Hicks

ISBN: 978-0-9824796-9-8
Library of Congress Control Number: 2011915778

Library of Congress subject headings:
1. Quilting – United States – History
2. African American quiltmakers
3. Patchwork - Patterns

Pattern concepts: Kyra E. Hicks

Pattern illustrations: Elyse Whittaker-Paek. See more of her work at www.elyse.biz.

Quilter: Carolyn L. Mazloomi. Visit www.CarolynLMazloomi.com.

Photographer: John Woo, a Washington, D.C. area freelance photographer.

Cover Design: ManjariGraphics

Interior Layout: Karen Krug. Visit www.PinnacleOfBrevard.com.

This book was created on a PC using Microsoft Word 2010. The interior font is Georgia, font size 12.

Scriptures taken from the Holy Bible, New International Version, Copyright © 1973, 1978, 1984 International Bible Society. Used by permission of Zondervan Bible Publishers.

This book is dedicated to:

Dr. James Washington, Jr.
New Grove Baptist Church
Winterville, GA

Deacon Jesse Porter, Jr.
Arlington, VA

Thank you both for your kindnesses, calls, prayers and coffee
- just when I needed it most.

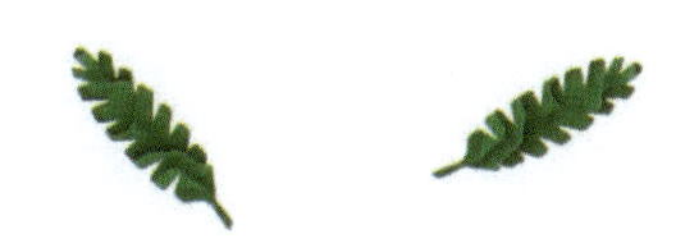

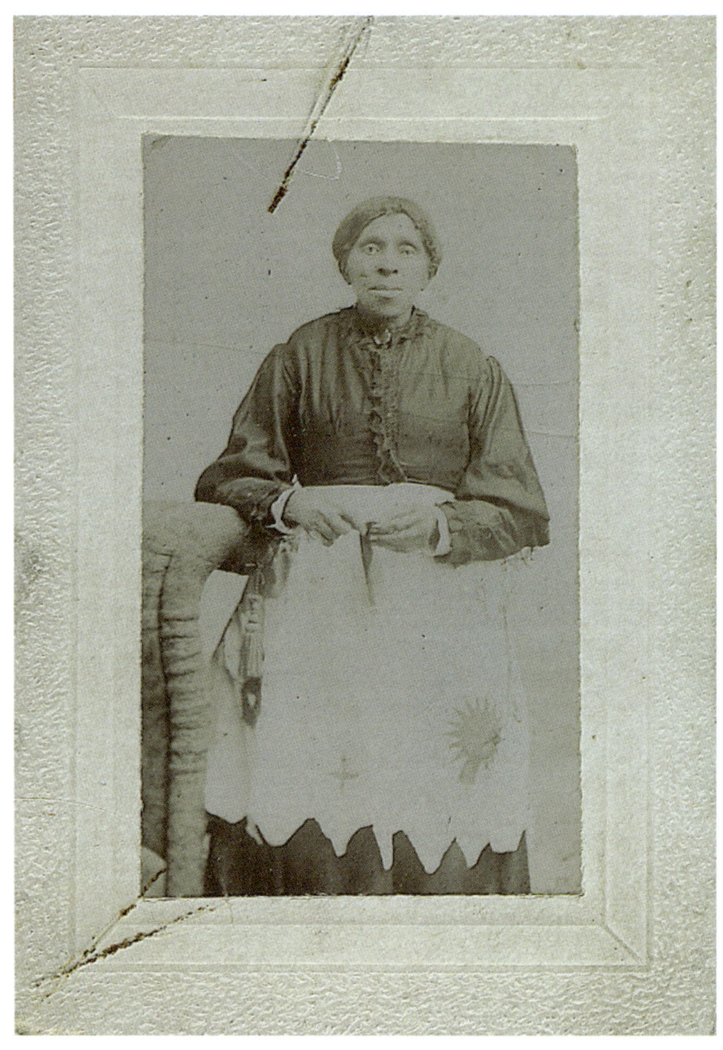

Harriet Powers, *carte de visite* circa 1895—1897
Charles F. McDannell photographer, McDannell Studio, 115 Broad St., Athens, GA
Courtesy of the Lee County Historical Society, Keokuk, IA

Harriet Powers' *Lord's Supper Quilt*

When I get to Heaven, I'm going to take a needle, a spool of thread, some cotton fabrics, and locate Mrs. Harriet Powers. I so yearn to spend a few hours just talking and sewing with her.

"Mrs. Powers," I'll ask in awe, "will you tell me about your quilts? How did you learn to create them? Who taught you? Where did you get the inspirations for your story quilts? How many did you stitch in your lifetime? What did Armsted, your husband, think about your quiltmaking? Did you teach your daughters, Amanda or Lizzie, or any of your twenty-or-so grandchildren to sew or quilt? Were there any local quilters whose work you respected?"

I'll keep pestering her. "Other than Atlanta and Athens, Georgia, where else were your quilts on display? How did you feel seeing your *Adam and Eve in the Garden of Eden* quilt at the 1895 Atlanta Cotton Exposition? Did you ever imagine that two of your quilts would still be admired and recognized more than 100 years after your passing?"

"Mrs. Powers," I'll finally ask, "what happened to your *Lord's Supper Quilt?*"

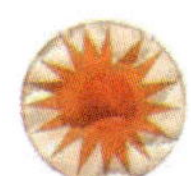

Harriet Powers was born a slave on October 29, 1837 in Madison County, just outside Athens, Georgia. Though we may never know for certain, she was most likely the unnamed 12-year-old girl listed in the 1850 Madison County, Georgia slave census as owned by Nancy Lester, a 65-year-old widow. A 45-year-old woman, also listed as owned by Mrs. Lester, could have been Mrs. Powers' mother.

Harriet married Armsted Powers, a farmer, in 1855. The couple had nine children, though only three survived to adulthood, according to the 1900 United States Census and Mrs. Powers' own words. These were: Amanda J. Powers Witcher (b. 1855), Alonzo Powers (b. 1860), and Marshall Powers (b. 1873).

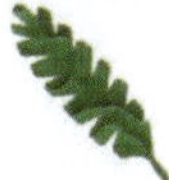

In 1886, Onieta Virginia "Jennie" Smith saw a Bible-themed quilt on display at the Northeast Georgia Fair held in Athens, Georgia. Jennie Smith, as she was known, was an art teacher at the Lucy Cobb Institute, a finishing school for young Southern white girls, in Athens. She eventually tracked down the quiltmaker, Harriet Powers, and offered to purchase the quilt. Mrs. Powers refused to sell the quilt, which she called *Adam and Eve in the Garden of Eden*, at any price.

In 1887, Mrs. Powers exhibited another quilt at the annual Northeast Georgia Colored Fair in Athens, where she won a "premium," or prize, for the piece.

By 1890, the Powers family was in financial difficulty, and Mrs. Powers sought out Jennie Smith to see if her offer to purchase the Bible-themed quilt was still open.

Miss Smith was indeed interested, but in a financial bind herself and could not complete the transaction. In 1891, Miss Smith sent notice to Mrs. Powers that she was then able to purchase the quilt, if it was still for sale. It was, and the two women arranged to meet in person. Mrs. Powers requested ten dollars for her quilt, but Miss Smith said she "only had five to give."

Mrs. Powers consulted with her husband, Armsted, and accepted the five dollars, about $120 in 2010 dollars, according to MeauringWorth.com.

Upon purchasing the quilt, Miss Smith did something incredible — she wrote down Mrs. Powers' descriptions of each of the blocks in the quilt. Can you imagine? Miss Smith, who still felt the pull of the quilt five years after first seeing it, documented Mrs. Powers' artistic thoughts and creative intentions. Miss Smith's handwritten notes are still available to read, by appointment, at the Smithsonian Institution in Washington, D.C., and are among rare insights directly from a former slave and nineteenth century woman artist.

Miss Smith later wrote of Mrs. Powers, "[a]fter giving me a full description of each scene with great earnestness, and deep piety she departed, but has been back several times to visit the darling offspring of her brain. She was only in a measure consoled for its loss when I promised to save her all my scraps."

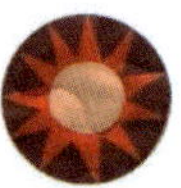

Jennie Smith submitted the Bible-themed *Adam and Eve in the Garden of Eden* quilt to be displayed during the 1895 Cotton States and International Exposition in Atlanta. Nearly 800,000 people from across the nation attended this Expo. Booker T. Washington, head of the famed Tuskegee Institute, was one of the opening-day speakers. The quilt, which was accepted, became part of an exhibit of slave-made items in the segregated Negro Building.

A well-off woman and award-winning quilter, Lorene Curtis Diver, and her husband traveled 740 miles from Keokuk, Iowa, to attend the Expo in Atlanta. A few years earlier, the Divers' only living child, a teenage girl, had passed away. As a tactic to work through her grief, Mrs. Diver learned photography. She took her camera to the Expo, and while visiting the popular Negro Building, she became captivated by Harriet Powers' Bible-themed quilt.

Mrs. Diver obtained permission to photograph the quilt, but she was not pleased with the image she made and employed a local, professional photographer to take a picture of the quilt. Mrs. Diver described the individual quilt blocks on the back of the sepia-toned picture. She also wrote that Mrs. Powers' idea behind stitching the quilt was to "'preach the gospel' in patchwork – tell the story of the fall of Adam & Eve..."

Mrs. Diver wanted to purchase this quilt, which we today call the *Bible Quilt*, but she was denied, presumably by Miss Jennie Smith.

I can only imagine that Mrs. Diver got in touch with Mrs. Powers directly and asked her about purchasing a quilt.

At the Lee County Historical Society in Keokuk, there is a file on Lorene Curtis Diver in the collection of the late local historian Raymond Everett Garrison. In this file is one of the 1895/96 photographs of the *Bible Quilt* with Mrs. Diver's handwritten descriptions, a copy of a letter from Miss Jennie Smith, a copy of a 1896 letter from Mrs. Harriet Powers, and an original *carte de visite* of Mrs. Powers.

Mrs. Powers' January 1896 letter reads, to me, as though she is presenting herself and her quiltmaking expertise for a potential artistic commission. She writes, in part:

"The life of Harriet Powers. Born in Madison Co. 8 miles from Athens on the Elberton road in the year Oct. 29, 1837. Her mistress was Nancy Lester. I commenced to learn at 11 years old and the white children learn me by sound on a poplar leaf. On Sundays after that I __ on books and done my own studying. I was married to Armsted Powers 1855. When I was free I moved to Dondy, Ga. In 1872 I made a quilt of 4 thousand and 50 diamonds.

"... In 1882 I became a member of Mt. Zion Baptist church. Then I visited Sunday school and read the Bible more than ever. Then I composed a quilt of the Lord's Supper from the New Testament. 2 thousand and 500 hundred diamonds.

"... I composed and completed the quilt of Adam and Eve in the Garden of Eden – afterward sold it to Miss. Jennie Smith, and it was represented by her at the Exposition at Atlanta. I was there at the Ex – Dec. 26, 189[5]."

There is no evidence, yet found, to indicate that Mrs. Diver actually commissioned or purchased a quilt from Mrs. Powers.

But, what if she did?

In 1917, Mrs. Diver suffered a bad fall down some stone steps that eventually left her blind. Her husband, James Diver, was said to have lovingly cared for her and "became her eyes" until she passed away in 1922.

Mr. Diver died in 1930, within a year of signing his last will and testament, in which he established the Lorene Curtis Diver Memorial Fund in honor of his wife and for the benefit of the Trinity Methodist Episcopal Church in Keokuk. Mr. Diver could not bear to dispose of his various properties, his home or the items that he and his wife had collected during their marriage. In the will, he left funds for a woman trustee to be appointed to live in the house, called Port Sunshine, and maintain it as it was – disposing of none of its treasures.

Mr. Diver's wishes were honored for many years. Amelia Buttschau Smith was the home's first trustee until her death in the mid-1950s. Subsequent trustees eventually received approval to sell various Diver properties. On September 19, 1959, thirty-seven years after the passing of Lorene Diver, the contents of Port Sunshine were sold in an auction.

I have yet to locate records from the 1959 auction – only an account of the auction's occurrence by local historian Raymond E. Garrison. It was Mr. Garrison's files that held the copy of the letter from Mrs. Powers as well as her photograph.

What if Lorene Diver had indeed commissioned a quilt from Harriet Powers? Again, *I have no evidence* that such an acquisition ever occurred.

But, again, what if she did?

Mr. Diver's will, recorded at the South Lee County Court and County Offices in Keokuk and witnessed by Katharyn Smith and Katherine E. Rankin, is a fascinating read. It is clear from the document that no household possession was to be discarded. I assume that would include a quilt.

I can imagine that Mrs. Diver, a wealthy woman and herself a quilter, was successful in acquiring a piece from Harriet Powers. I imagine the quilt would likely have been a pictorial, Bible-themed one.

I can also imagine that this pictorial quilt would have survived Mrs. Diver's passing and remained in Port Sunshine with all her other household treasures until that 1959 auction in Keokuk.

I can just imagine.

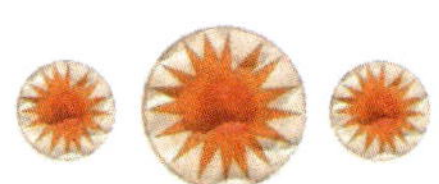

I am intrigued by the idea that a quilt by Mrs. Powers still exists in private hands. Today, two of Mrs. Powers' quilts (of which we are aware) have survived – passed through the decades by love of the quilts' unique, storytelling qualities. The *Bible Quilt* is now owned by the Smithsonian Institution National Museum of American History. A second quilt, which also includes Bible stories, is now called the *Pictorial Quilt* and is owned by the Museum of Fine Arts, Boston. I think it is miraculous that two quilts, *stitched by the same former slave*, could independently find homes in major cultural centers.

What happened to the 1882 Lord's Supper quilt that Mrs. Powers mentioned in her letter to Mrs. Diver?

What would such a quilt look like?

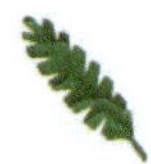

The *Lord's Supper Quilt* designed here was indeed inspired by Mrs. Powers' known quilts. Mrs. Powers read the Bible and attended Sunday school so I designed quilt blocks of popular Bible stories that may have been taught in those Sunday classes. I have also included a personally meaningful Bible story in one block.

I assume Mrs. Powers named her piece the *Adam and Eve in the Garden of Eden* quilt because the couples are in the first block in the upper left – leading the quilt narrative. As a result, the Lord's Supper is illustrated in the first block on this piece.

Additionally, Mrs. Powers seemed to find three stories important enough to repeat in her two known, surviving quilts. I assume she would have repeated them in the *Lord's Supper Quilt*. These blocks represent:

- Adam and Eve being tempted by the serpent - Sin
- Jesus being baptized by John - Salvation
- Jesus and the two thieves being crucified - Redemption

With the exception of the Lord's Supper block, each block is in the order it appears in the Old and New Testaments, from the Creation to the Accession.

In September 2002, Rev. Stephanie Jennings-Stratford of Capital Heights, MD, visited Mount Zion Baptist Church in Arlington, Virginia, for a series of revival sermons. One sermon, titled "Why Are You Laughing?" had a profound impact on me. Rev. Jennings shared the story of Sarah chuckling after overhearing the Lord tell Abraham that his elderly, barren wife would give birth to a son. "How impossible is that?" Sarah, who would become the mother of Isaac, may have smirked to herself. When my faith wavers, I listen to the cassette tape of Rev. Jennings reminding me of God's awesome power to move in our lives despite our past behaviors, our present circumstances or how long it has been since we've yearned for that thing we've asked of God. I am convinced that if Mrs. Powers had heard Rev. Jennings preach that winter night, she would have sewn a block featuring Sarah and Abraham, too.

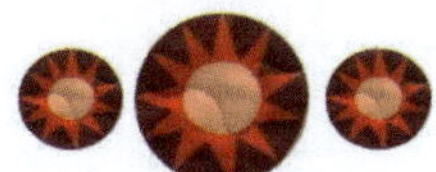

In 1991, Sotheby's sold the most expensive quilt at auction, the *Reconciliation Quilt*, a Civil-War era piece completed in 1867 by Lucinda Ward Honstain, for $264,000.

I can imagine that in 1959, a quilt stitched by Mrs. Powers was sold at a Keokuk, Iowa auction for some modest amount. The quilt would not have had Mrs. Powers name embroidered or signed on to it. Only the distinctive Bible-themed cotton story blocks and similarities to her two surviving quilts would mark the piece. Maybe someone who sees this *Lord's Supper Quilt* will be moved to look in a guest room closet or inside an old cedar chest to see if that antique religious quilt that's been in the family for years might just be....

I can only imagine.

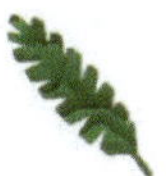

This pattern can be reduced to make a miniature quilt or enlarged to make a wall-hanging or bed-sized quilt. It is up to you!

I would like to thank illustrator Elyse Whittaker-Paek for taking my rough sketches and notes and channeling Mrs. Powers as she drew these quilt block patterns. I am also thankful to Dr. Carolyn L. Mazloomi for being so supportive of this project that she made the *Lord's Supper Quilt* photographed here.

Enjoy!
Kyra E. Hicks

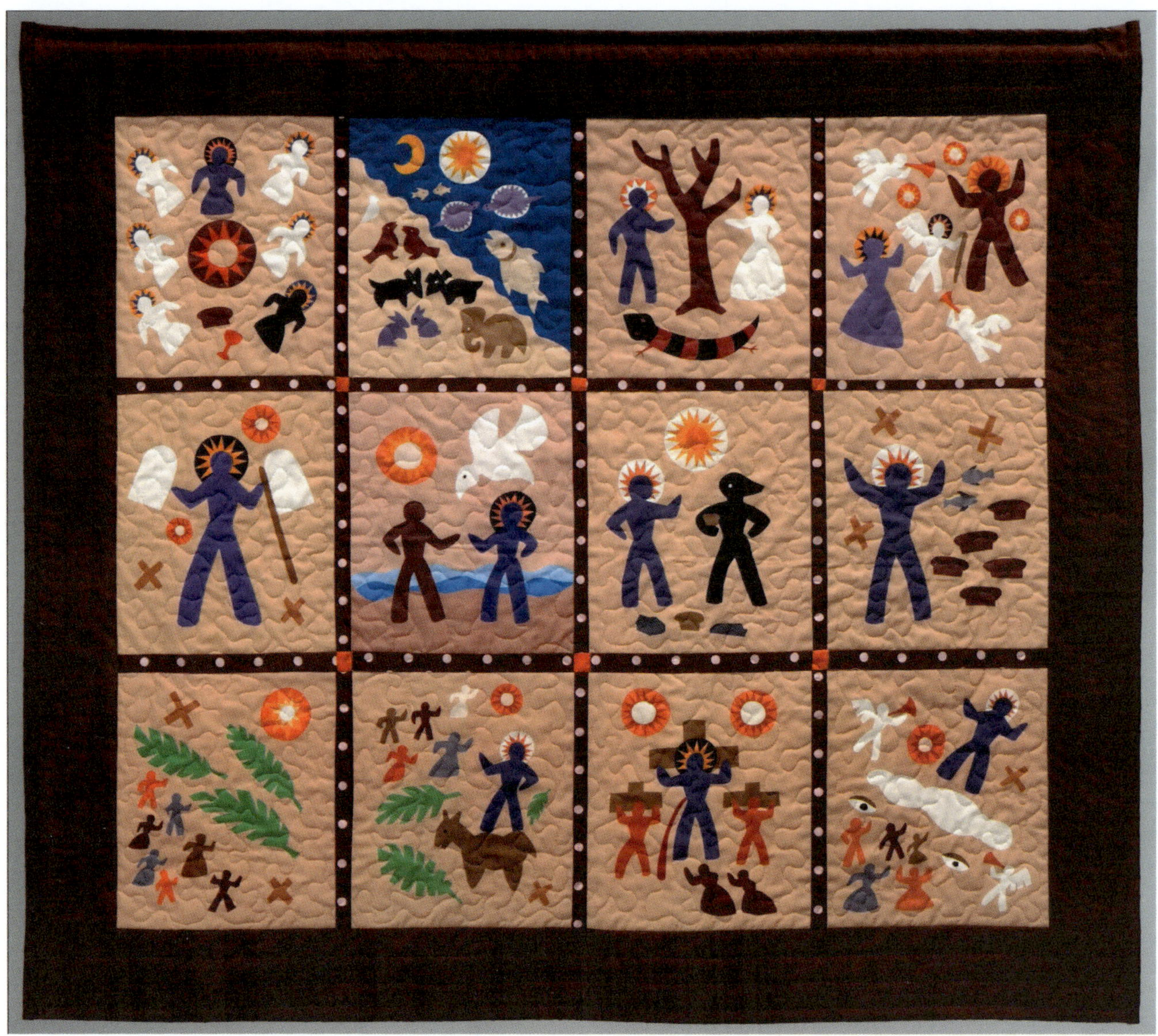

The Lord's Supper Quilt
By Kyra E. Hicks

1. The Lord's Supper
2. The Creation
3. Adam and Eve and the Tree of Knowledge of Good and Evil
4. Sarah and Abraham Visited by Three Angles
5. Moses and the Ten Commandments
6. John Baptizing Jesus – God is Well Pleased
7. The Devil Tries to Tempt Jesus
8. Jesus Gives Thanks and Feeds More Than 5,000
9. The Road to Jerusalem
10. Jesus' Triumphant Entry
11. The Crucifixion
12. The Accession

The Lord's Supper Quilt Pieces

	Jesus w/Crown	Men	Women	Angels	Crosses	Stars	Animals	Misc.
Lord's Supper	1	6				1		1 Bread 1 Wine
The Creation						1	13	1 Moon
Adam & Eve		1	1				1	1 Tree
Sarah & Abraham		1	1	3		3		1 Staff
Moses		1			2	2		1 Staff 2 Tablets
John & Jesus	1	1				1	1	2 Waves
The Devil & Jesus	1	1				1		2 Loaves 2 Rocks
Jesus Feeds	1				3		2	5 Loaves
The Road		4	3		2	1		3 Leaves
Jesus' Entry	1	2	3		1	1		3 Leaves
The Crucifixion	1	2	2		3	2		Blood
The Accession	1	2	3	2	1	1		2 Eyes
Total Pieces by Type	**7**	**21**	**13**	**5**	**12**	**14**	**17**	**28**

Blocks		12
Sashing		17
Tiny Squares		6
Border		4
Backing		1
Grand Total:		157

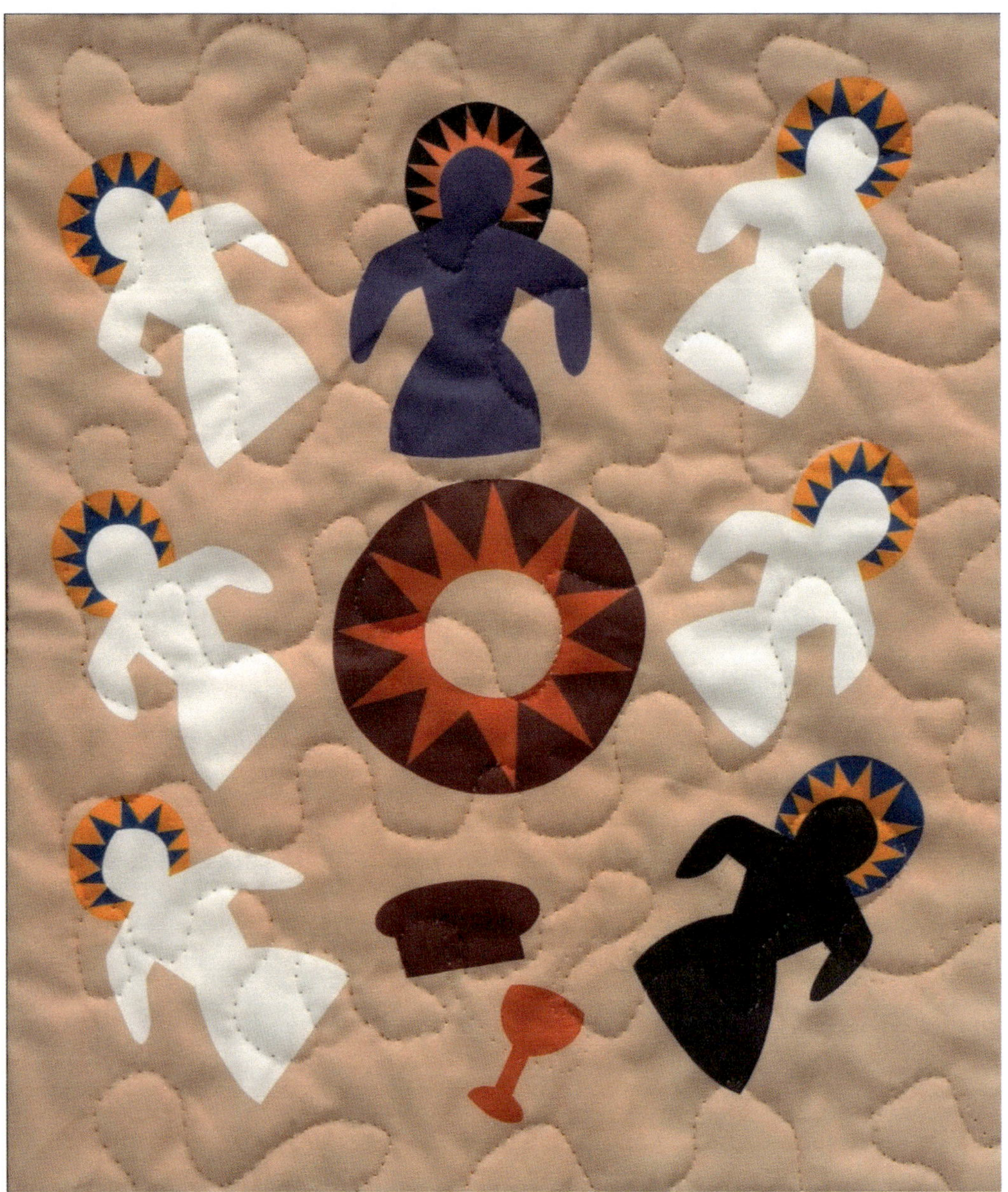

Block 1 - The Lord's Supper
Matthew 26: 26 – 29

While they were eating, Jesus took bread, gave thanks and broke it, and gave it to his disciples, saying, "Take and eat; this is my body."

Then he took the cup, gave thanks and offered it to them, saying, "Drink from it, all of you. This is my blood of the covenant, which is poured out for many for the forgiveness of sins. I tell you, I will not drink of this fruit of the vine from now on until that day when I drink it anew with you in my Father's kingdom.

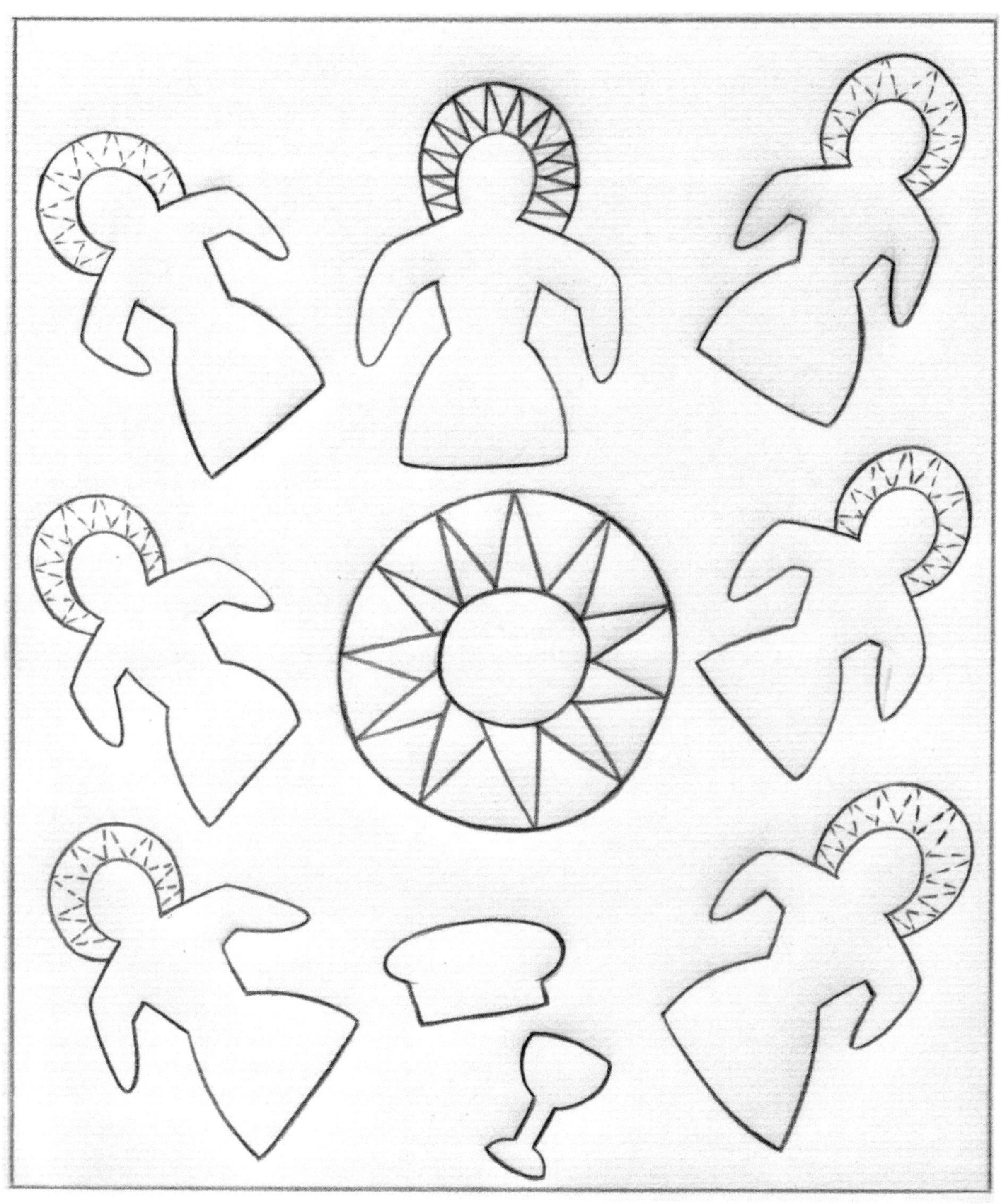

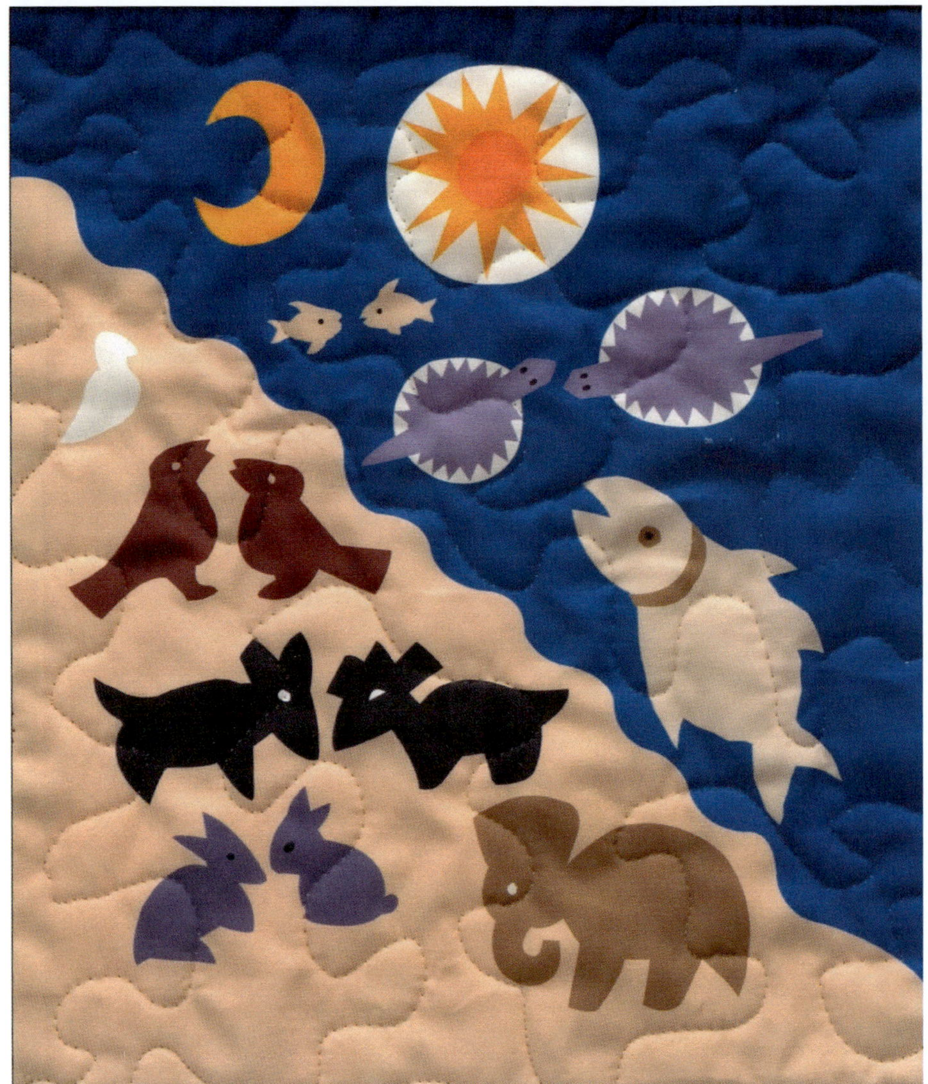

Block 2 - The Creation
Genesis 1: 1-2, 20 - 21, 24 - 25

In the beginning God created the heavens and the earth. Now the earth was formless and empty, darkness was over the surface of the deep, and the Spirit of God was hovering over the waters....

And God said, "Let the water teem with living creatures, and let birds fly above the earth across the expanse of the sky." So God created the great creatures of the sea and every living and moving thing with which the water teems, according to their kinds, and every winged bird according to its kind. And God saw that it was good....

And God said, "Let the land produce living creatures according to their kinds: livestock, creatures that move along the ground, and wild animals, each according to its kind." And it was so. God made the wild animals according to their kinds, the livestock according to their kinds, and all the creatures that move along the ground according to their kinds. And God saw that it was good.

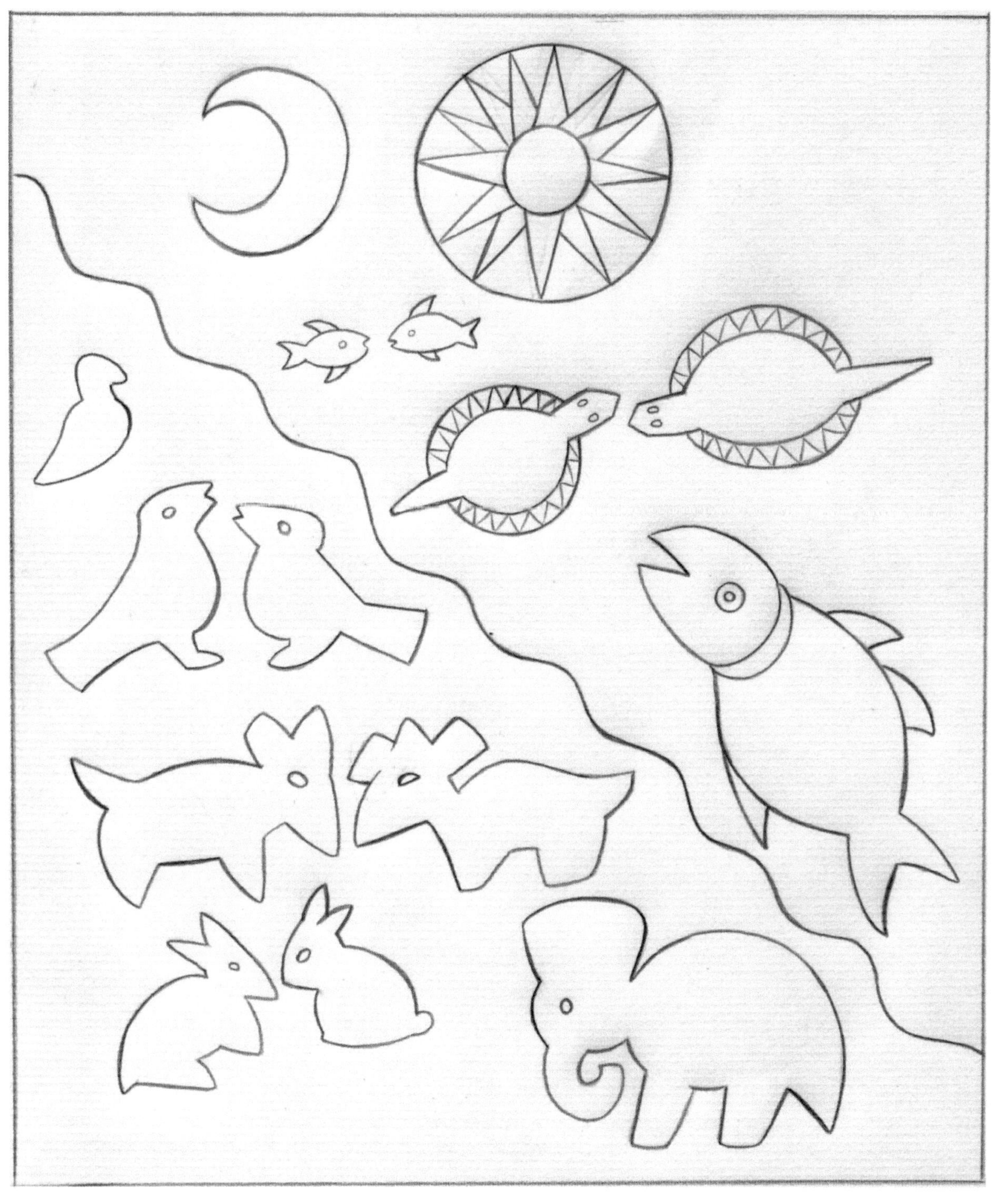

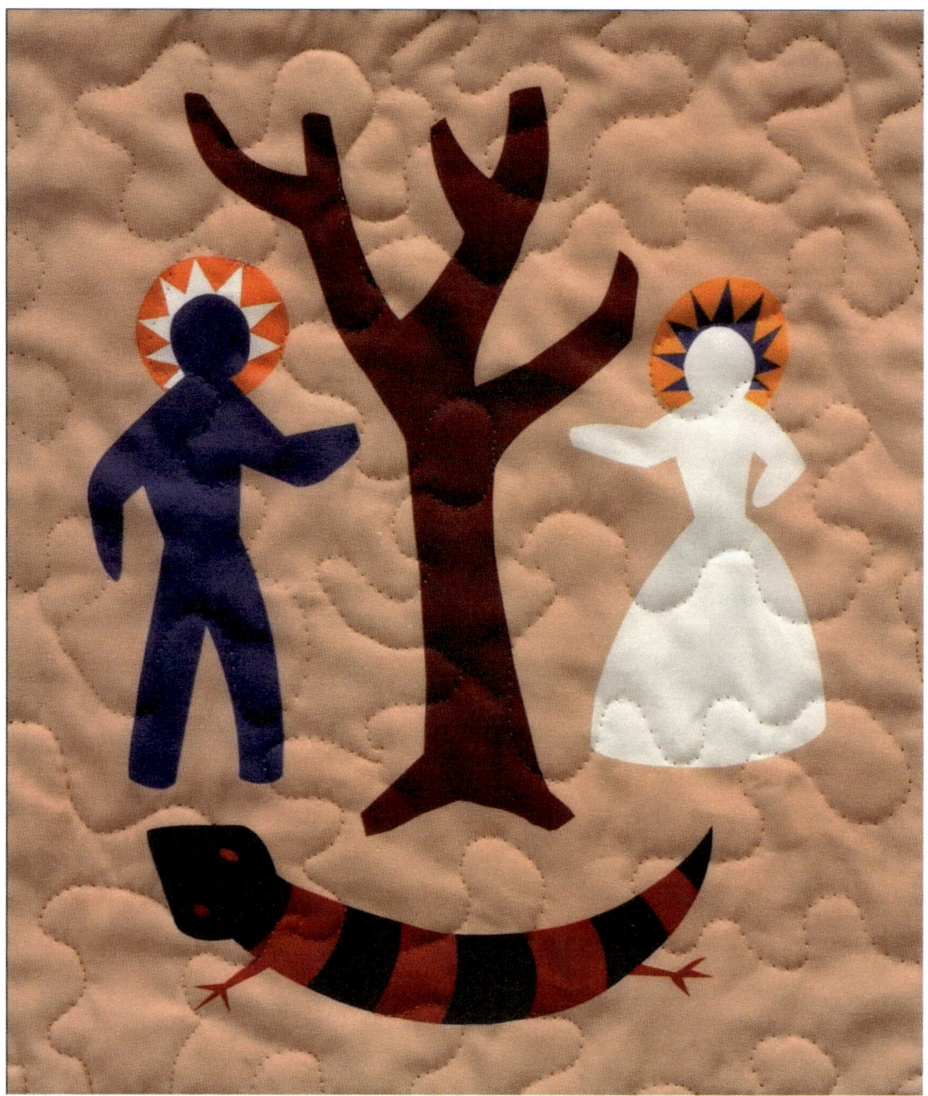

Block 3 – Adam and Eve and the Tree of Knowledge of Good and Evil
Genesis 2: 8-9, 15 – 17, Genesis 3:1

Now the Lord God had planted a garden in the east, in Eden; and there he put the man he had formed. And the Lord God made all kinds of trees grow out of the ground – trees that were pleasing to the eye and good for food. In the middle of the garden were the tree of life and the tree of the knowledge of good and evil....

The Lord God took the man and put him in the Garden of Eden to work it and take care of it. And the Lord God commanded the man, "You are free to eat from any tree in the garden; but you must not eat from the tree of the knowledge of good and evil, for when you eat of it you will surely die....

Now the serpent was more crafty than any of the wild animals the Lord God had made. He said to the woman, "Did God really say, 'You must not eat from any tree in the garden'?

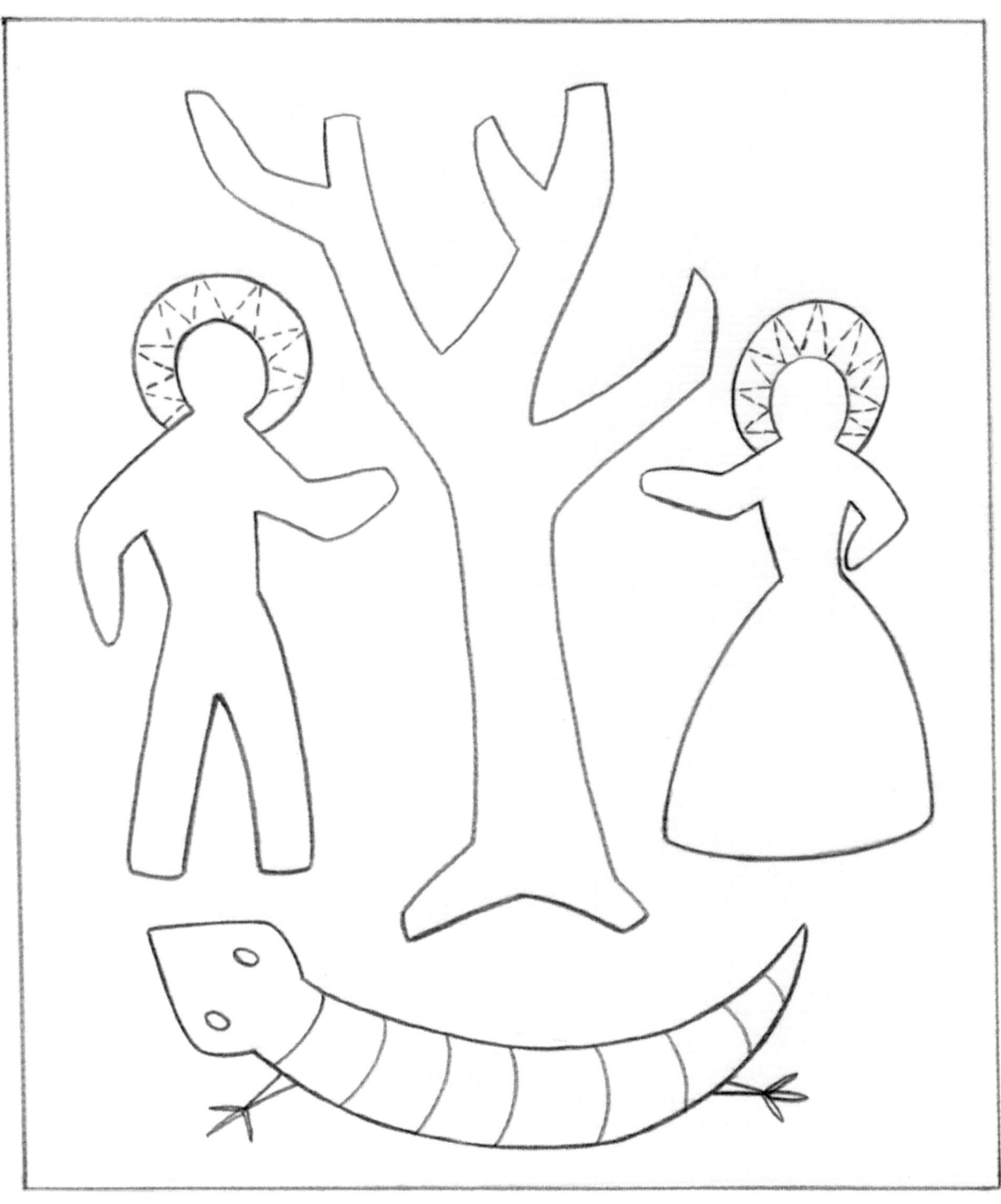

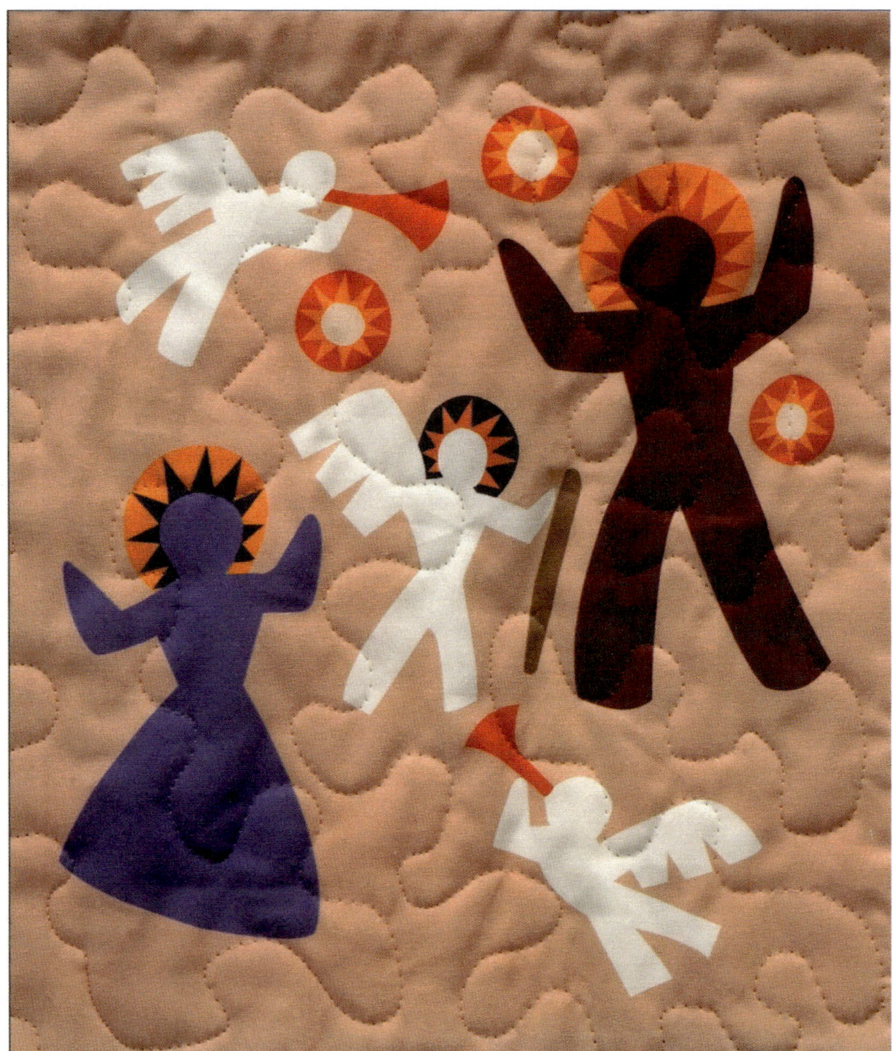

Block 4 – Sarah and Abraham Visited by Three Angles
Genesis 18:2, 9 – 14a

Abraham looked up and saw three men standing nearby. When he saw them, he hurried from the entrance of his tent to meet them and bowed low to the ground....

"Where is your wife Sarah?" they asked him.

"There, in the tent," he said.

Then the Lord said, "I will surely return to you about this time next year, and Sarah your wife will have a son."

Now Sarah was listening at the entrance to the tent, which was behind him. Abraham and Sarah were already old and well advanced in years, and Sarah was past the age of childbearing. So Sarah laughed to herself as she thought, "After I am worn out and my master is old, will I now have this pleasure?"

Then the Lord said to Abraham, "Why did Sarah laugh and say, 'Will I really have a child now that I am old?' Is anything too hard for the Lord?..."

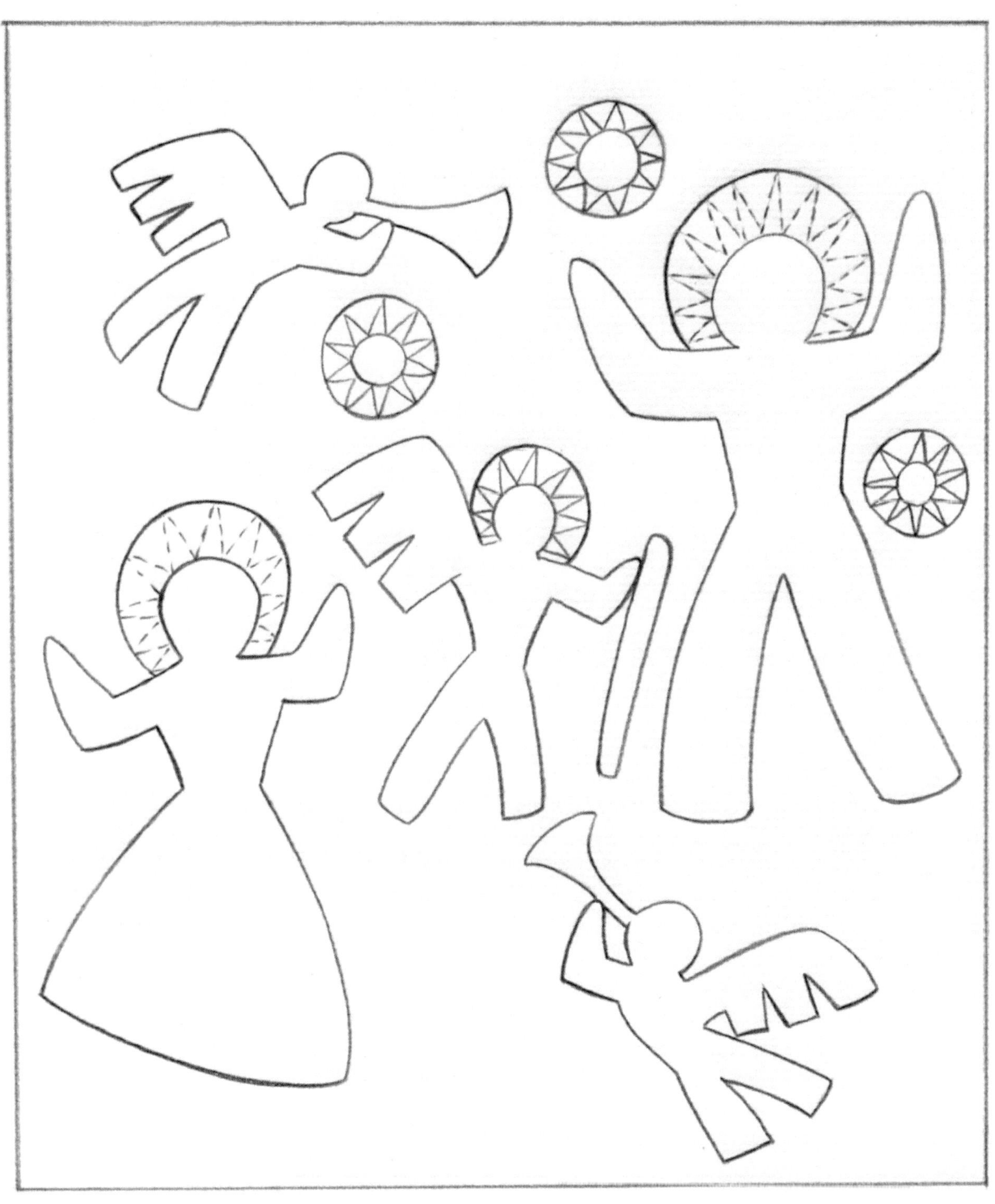

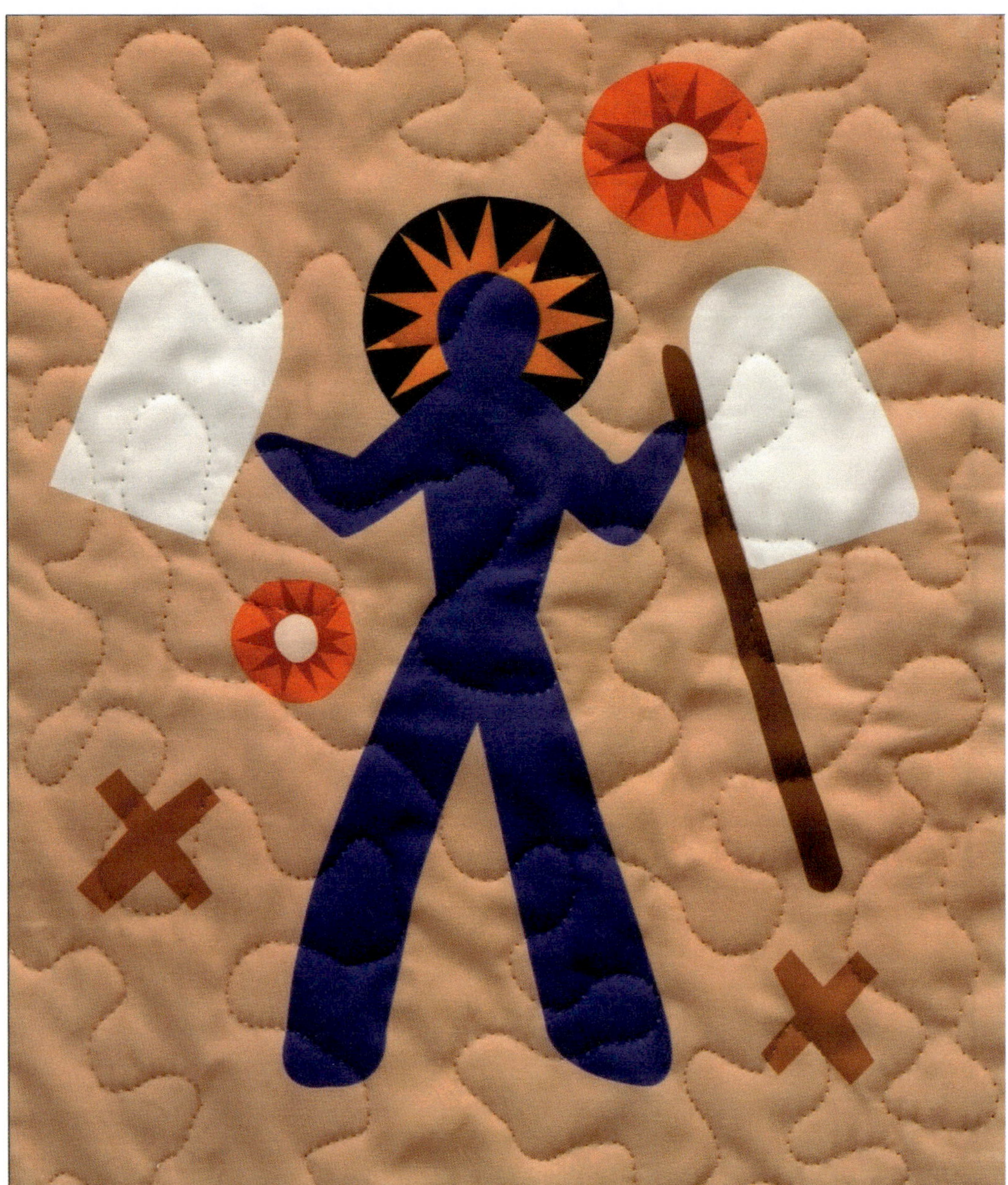

Block 5 – Moses and the Ten Commandments
Exodus 19:5-6, 34:27-28

Now if you obey me fully and keep my covenant, then out of all nations you will be my treasured possession. Although the whole earth is mine, you will be for me a kingdom of priests and a holy nation. These are the words you are to speak to the Israelites....

Then the Lord said to Moses, "Write down these words, for in accordance with these words I have made a covenant with you and with Israel." Moses was there with the Lord forty days and forty nights without eating bread or drinking water. And he wrote on the tablets the words of the covenant – the Ten Commandments.

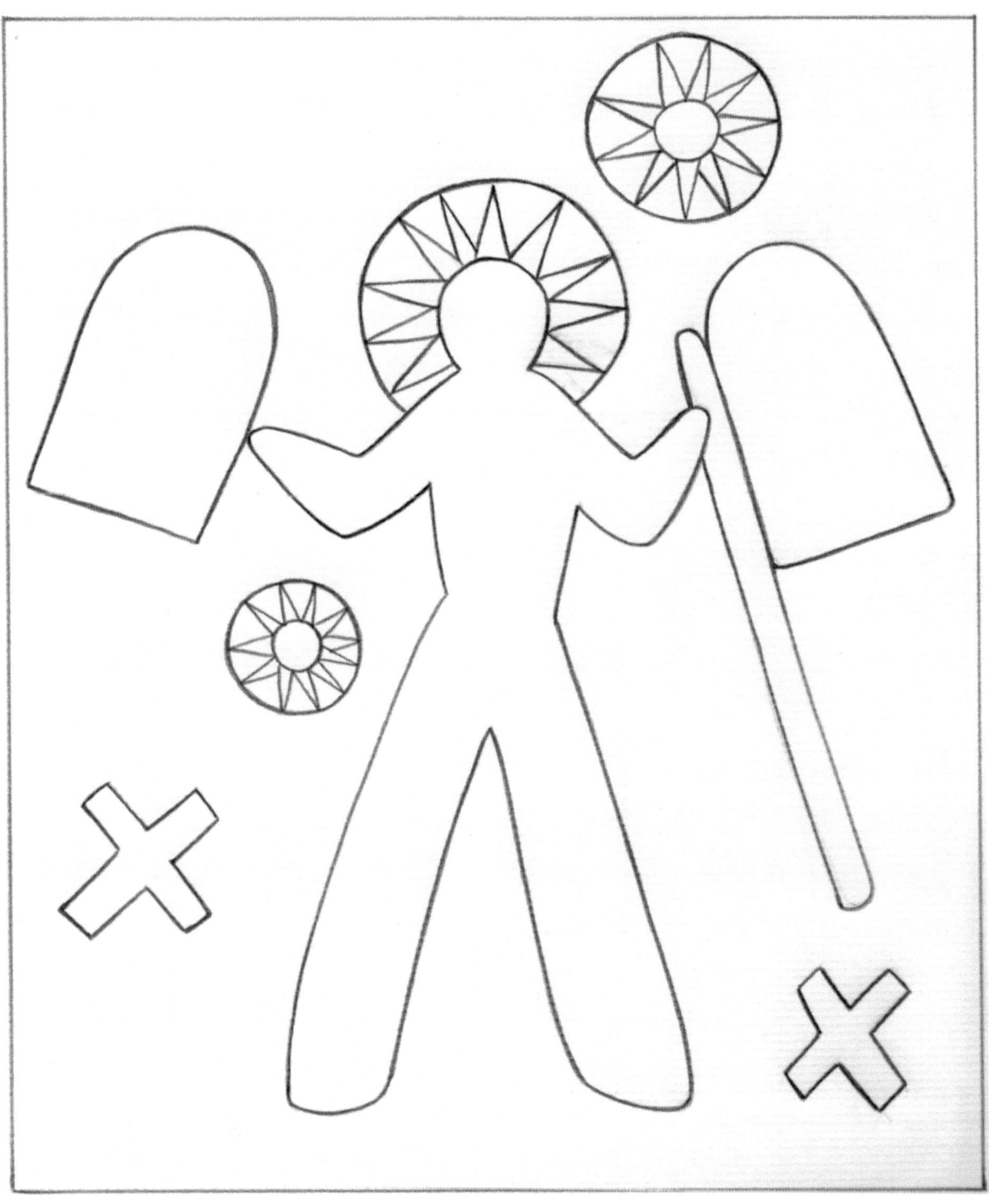

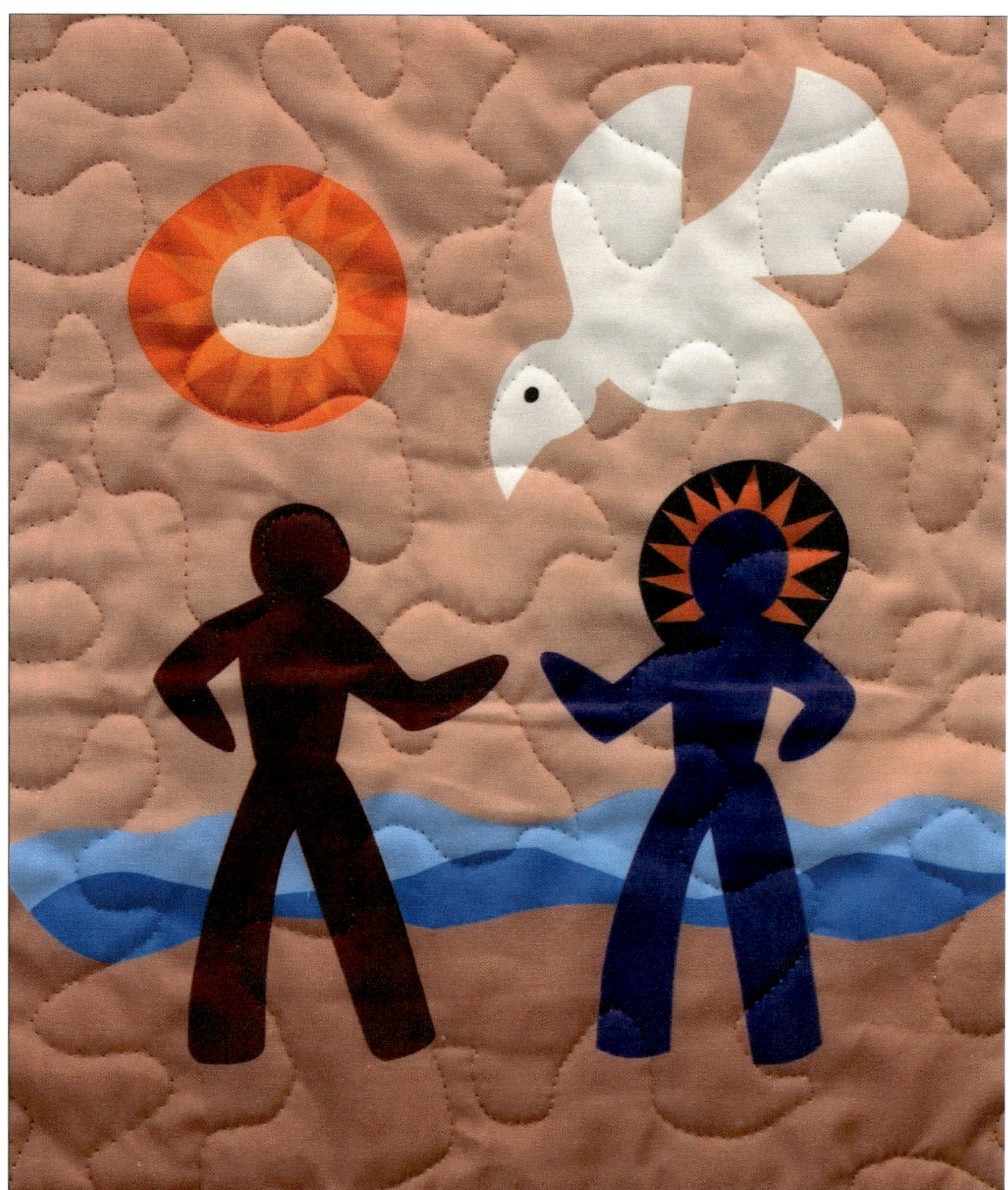

Block 6 – John Baptizing Jesus, God is Well Pleased
Luke 3: 21-22

When all the people were being baptized, Jesus was baptized too. And as he was praying, heaven was opened and the Holy Spirit descended on him in bodily form like a dove. And a voice came from heaven: "You are my Son, whom I love; with you I am well pleased."

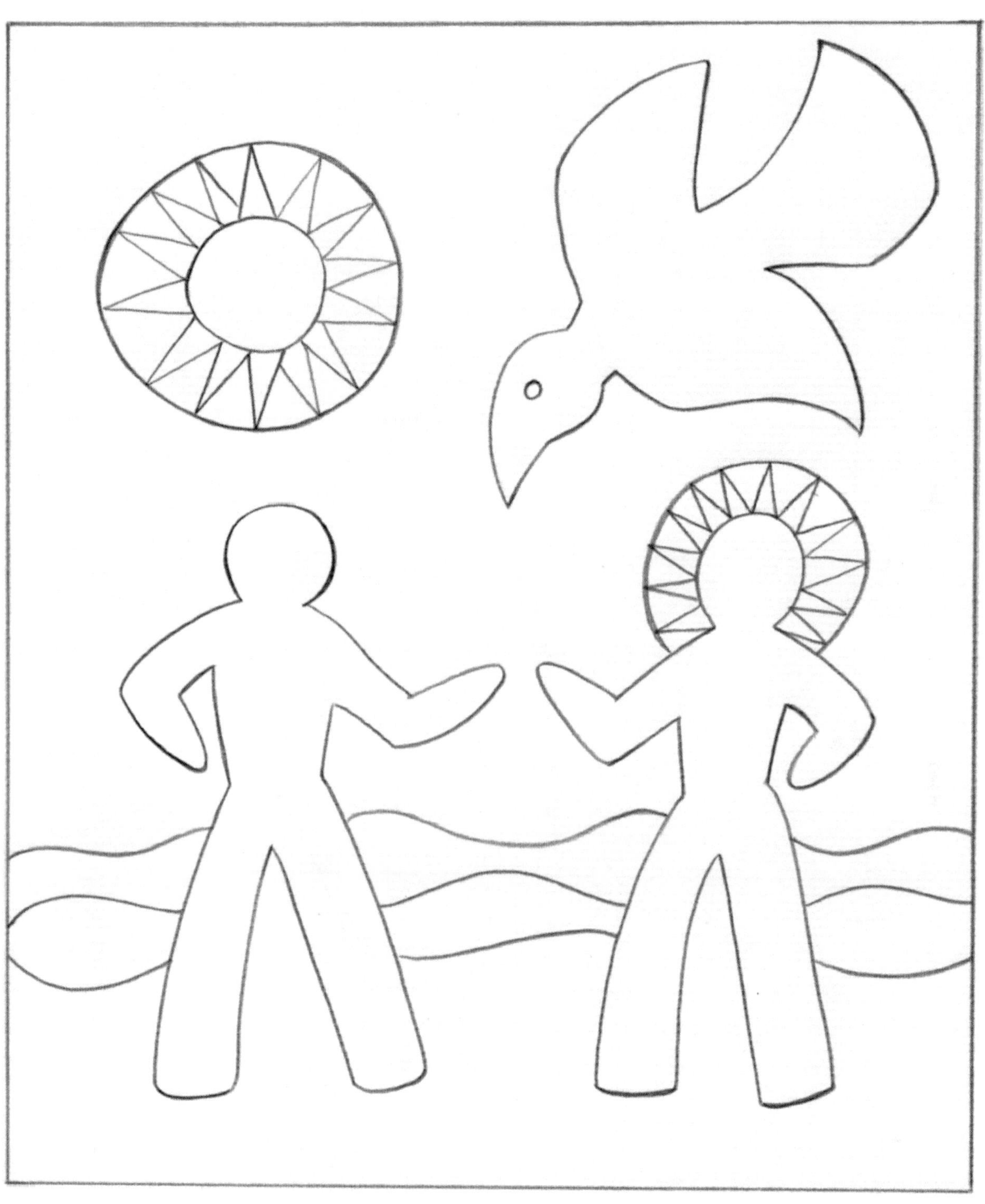

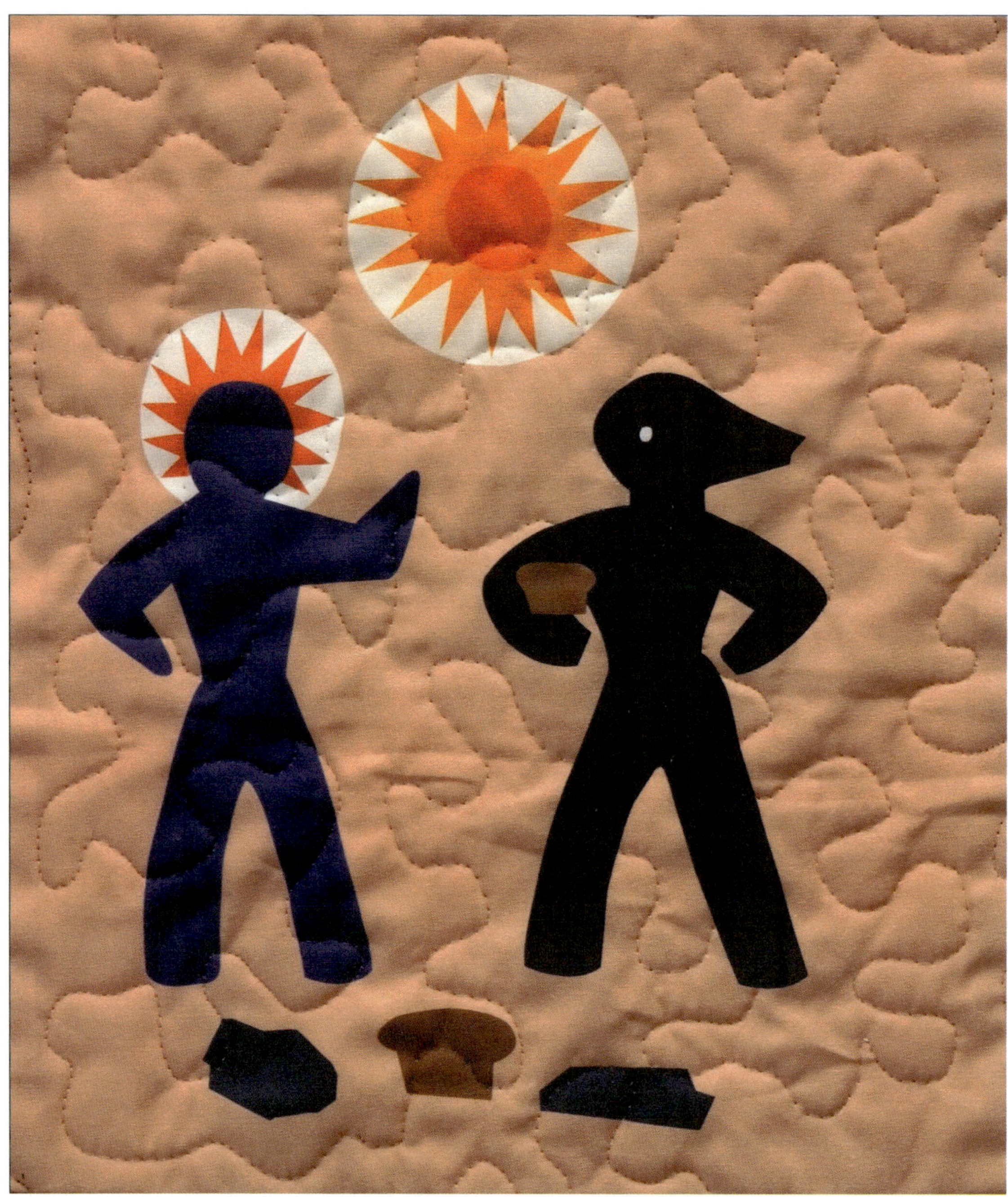

Block 7 – The Devil Tries to Tempt Jesus
Matthew 4:1-4

Then Jesus was led by the Spirit into the wilderness to be tempted by the devil. After fasting forty days and forty nights, he was hungry. The tempter came to him and said, "If you are the Son of God, tell these stones to become bread."

Jesus answered, "It is written: 'Man does not live on bread alone, but on every word that comes from the mouth of God.'

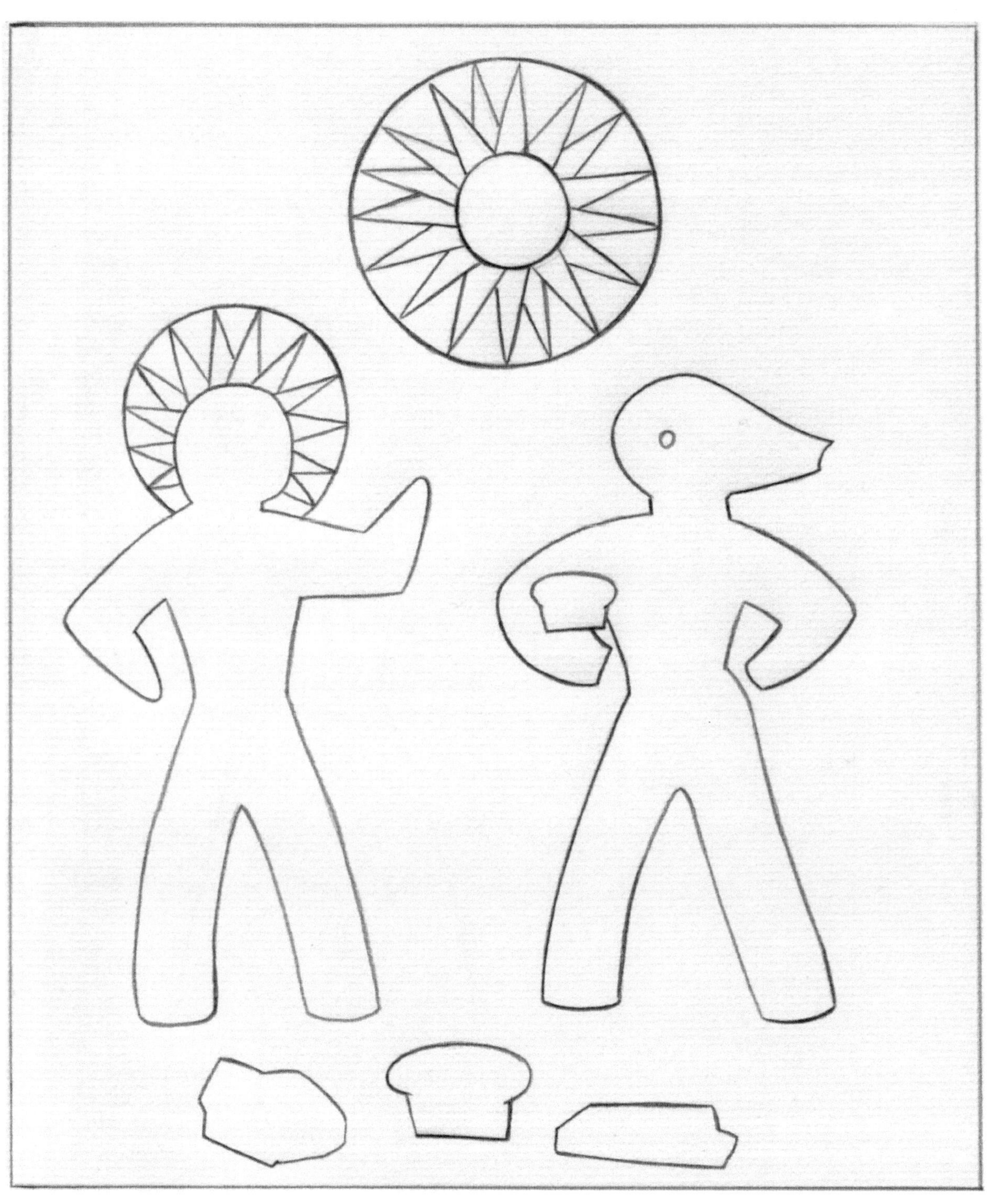

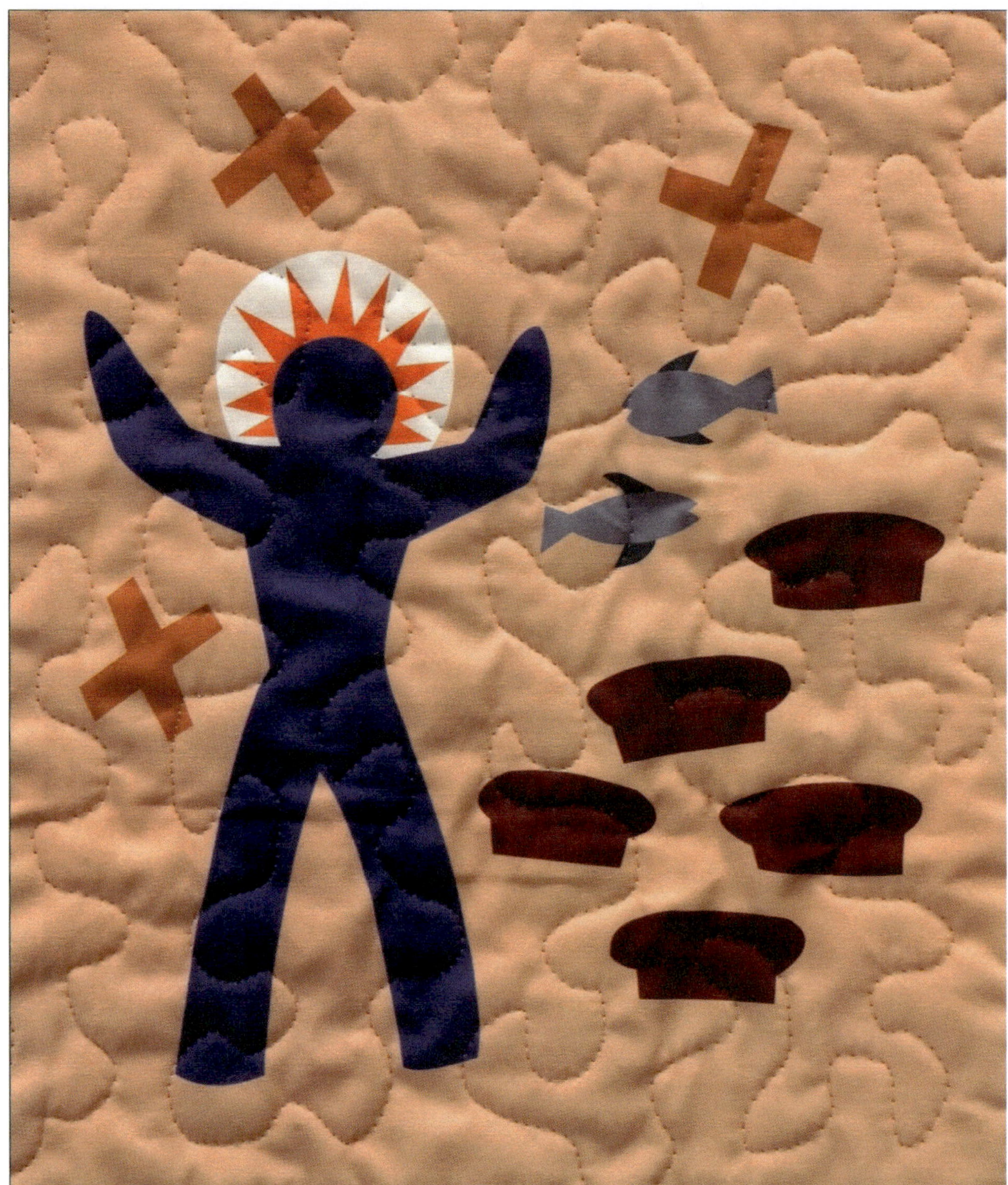

Block 8 – Jesus Gives Thanks and Feeds More Than 5,000
Matthew 14: 17-21

"We have here only five loaves of bread and two fish," they answered.

"Bring them here to me," he said. And he directed the people to sit down on the grass. Taking the five loaves and the two fish and looking up to heaven, he gave thanks and broke the loaves. Then he gave them to the disciples, and the disciples gave them to the people. They all ate and were satisfied, and the disciples picked up twelve basketfuls of broken pieces that were left over. The number of those who ate was about five thousand men, besides women and children.

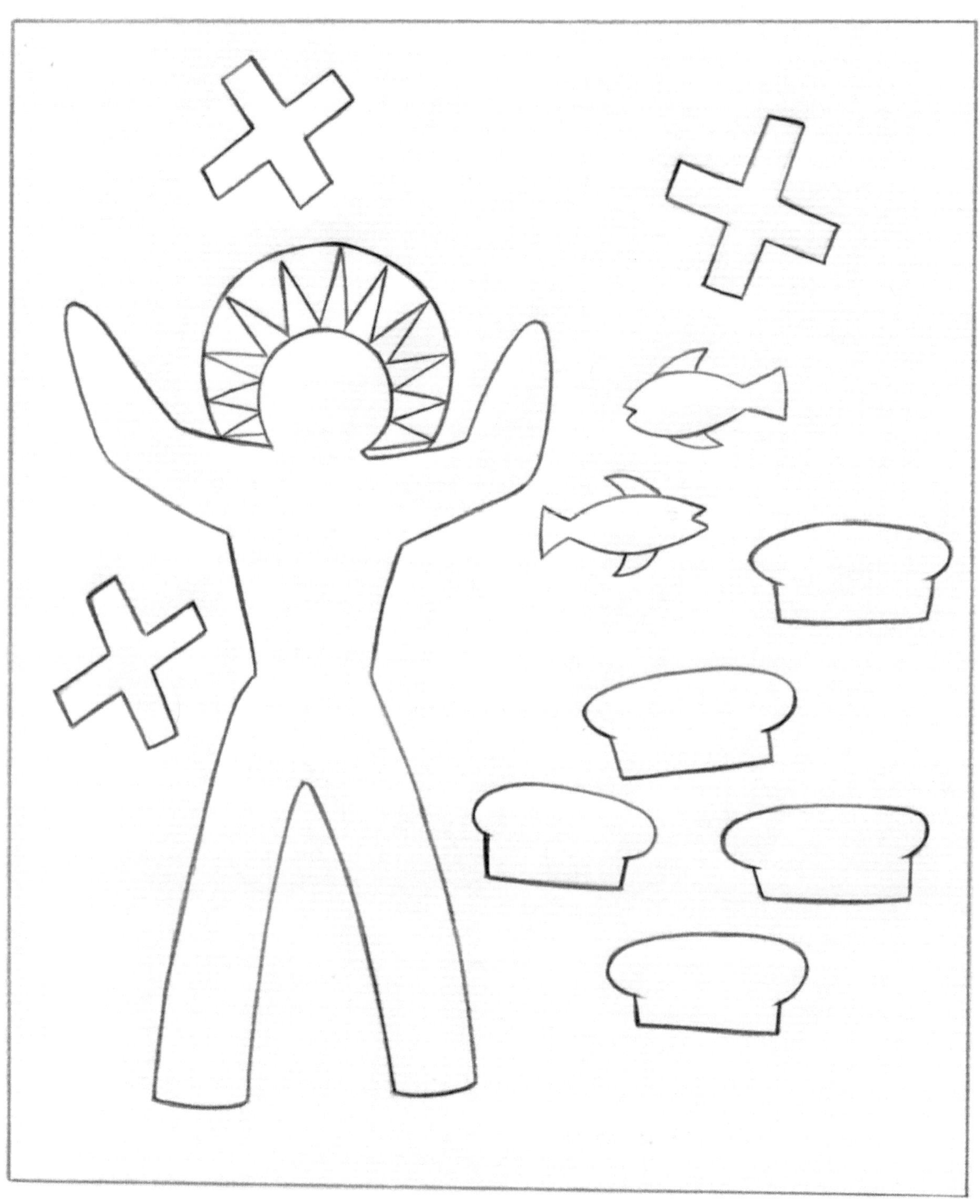

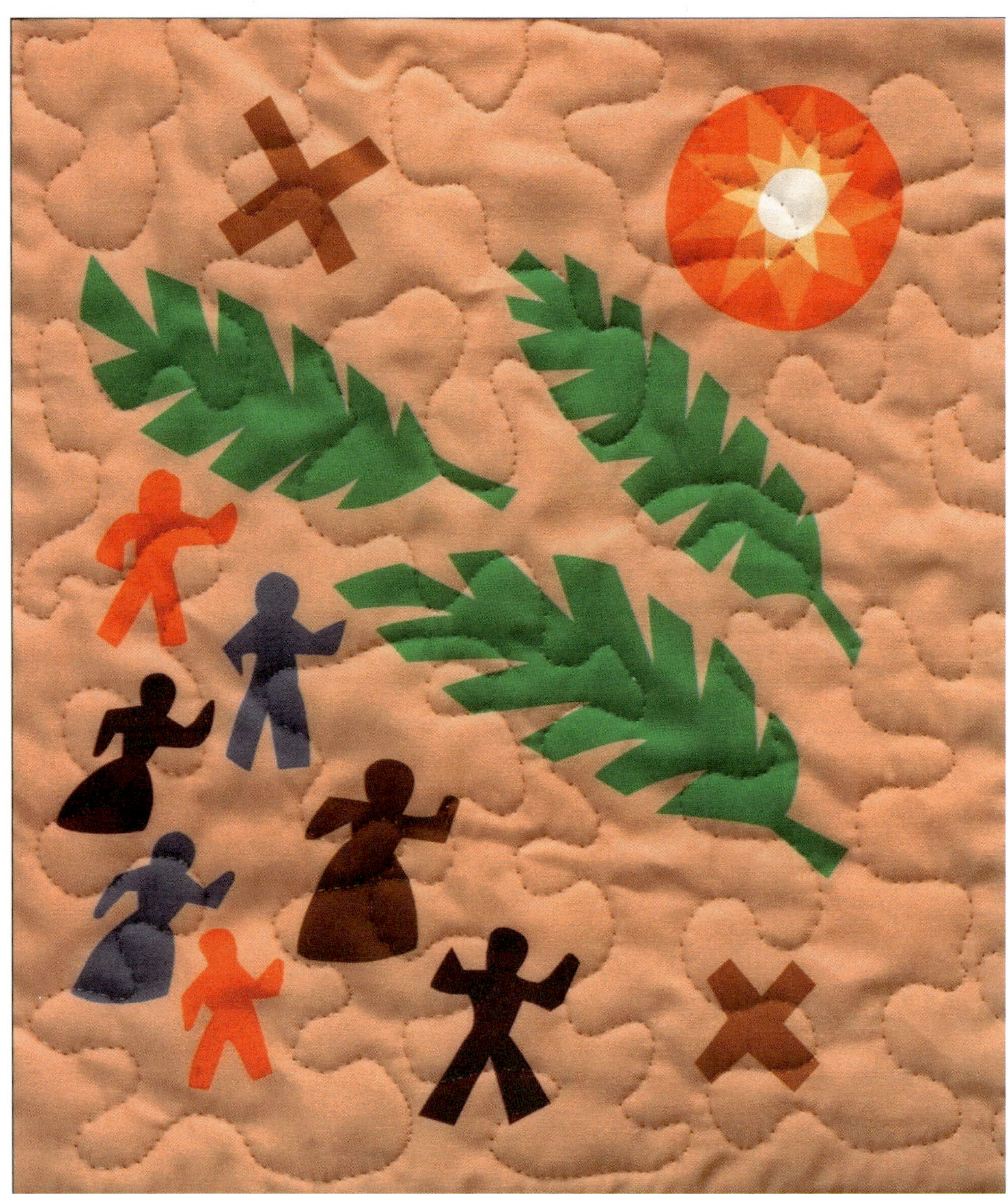

Block 9 – The Road to Jerusalem
Matthew 21: 8 - 9

A very large crowd spread their cloaks on the road, while others cut branches from the trees and spread them on the road. The crowds that went ahead of him and those that followed shouted,

"Hosanna to the Son of David!"

"Blessed is he who comes in the name of the Lord!"

"Hosanna in the highest!"

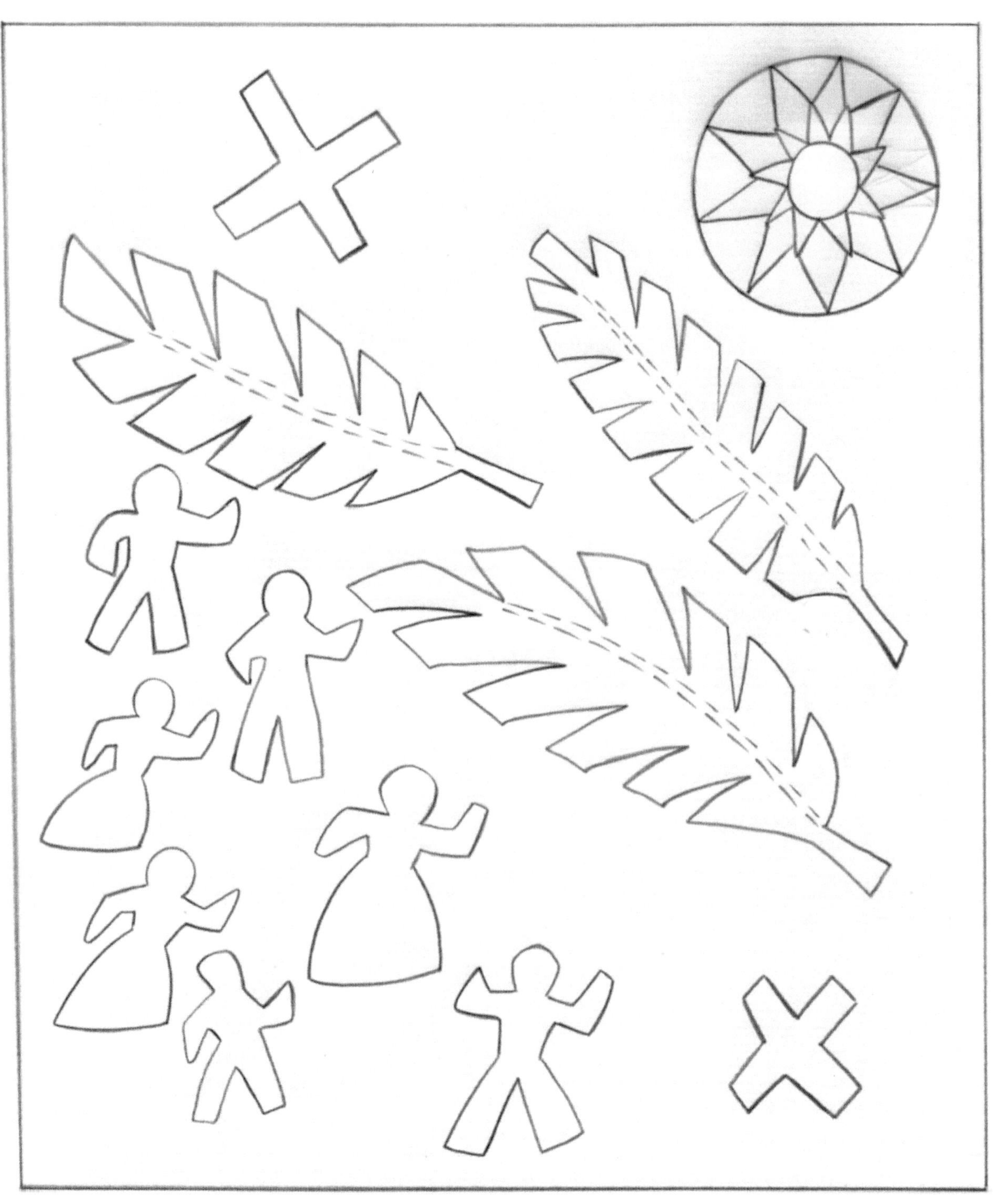

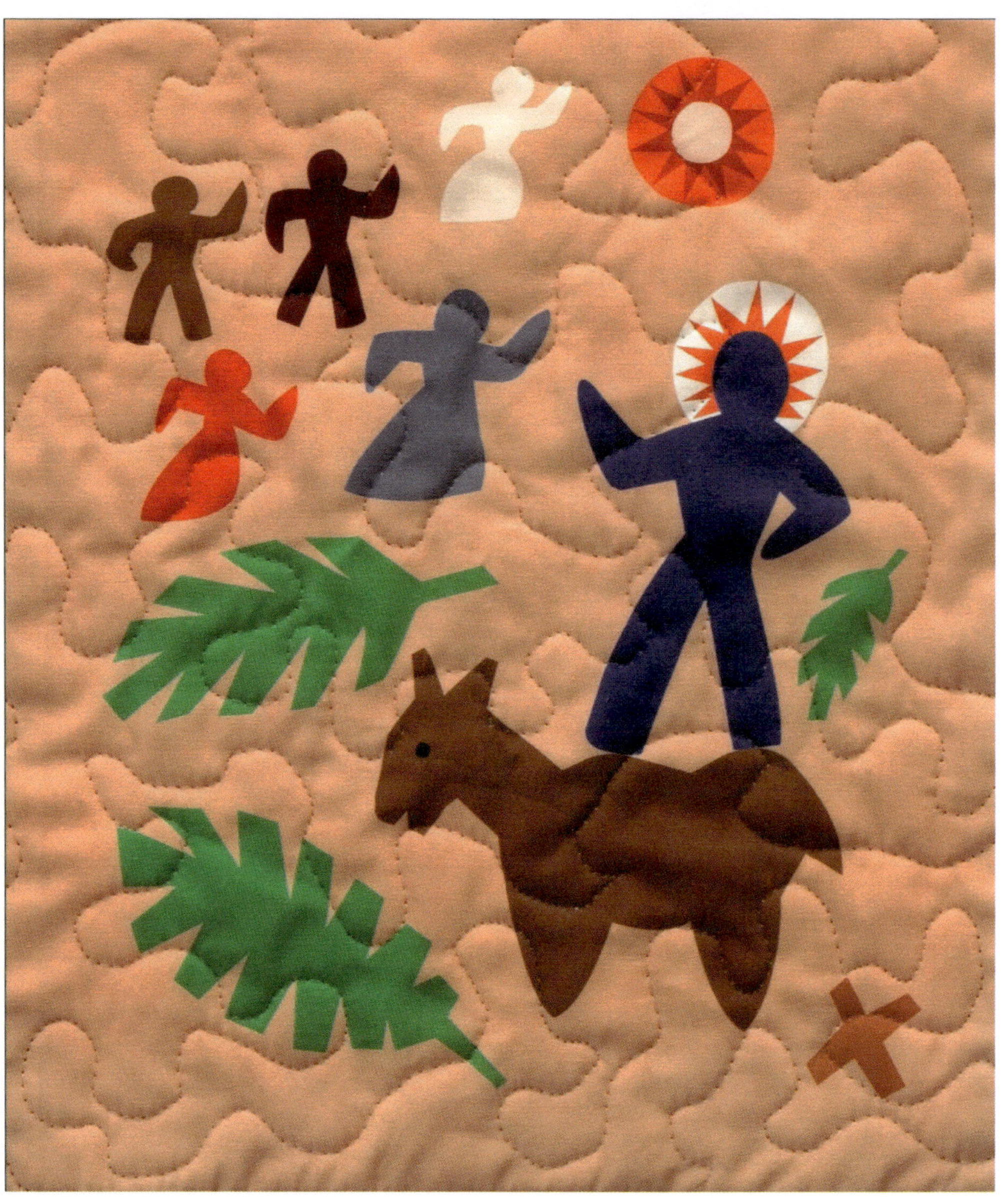

Block 10 – Jesus' Triumphant Entry
Mark 11: 1 – 4a, 7 - 8

As they approached Jerusalem and came to Bethphage and Bethany at the Mount of Olives, Jesus sent two of his disciples, saying to them, "Go to the village ahead of you, and just as you enter it, you will find a colt tied there, which no one has ever ridden. Untie it and bring it here. If anyone asks you, 'Why are you doing this?' tell him, 'The Lord needs it and will send it back here shortly.'"

They went and found a colt outside in the street, tied at a doorway.... When they brought the colt to Jesus and threw their cloaks over it, he sat on it. Many people spread their cloaks on the road, while others spread branches they had cut in the fields.

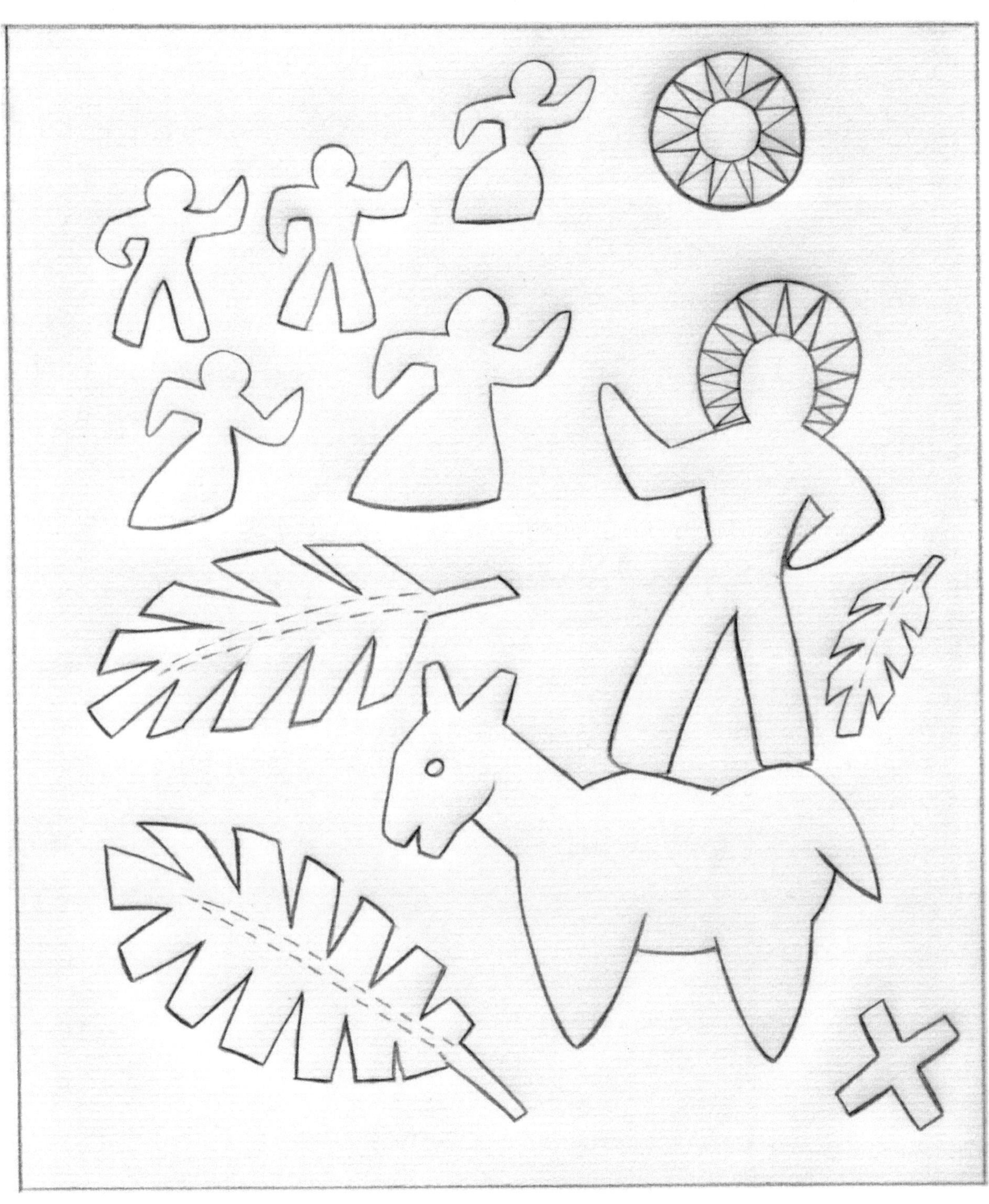

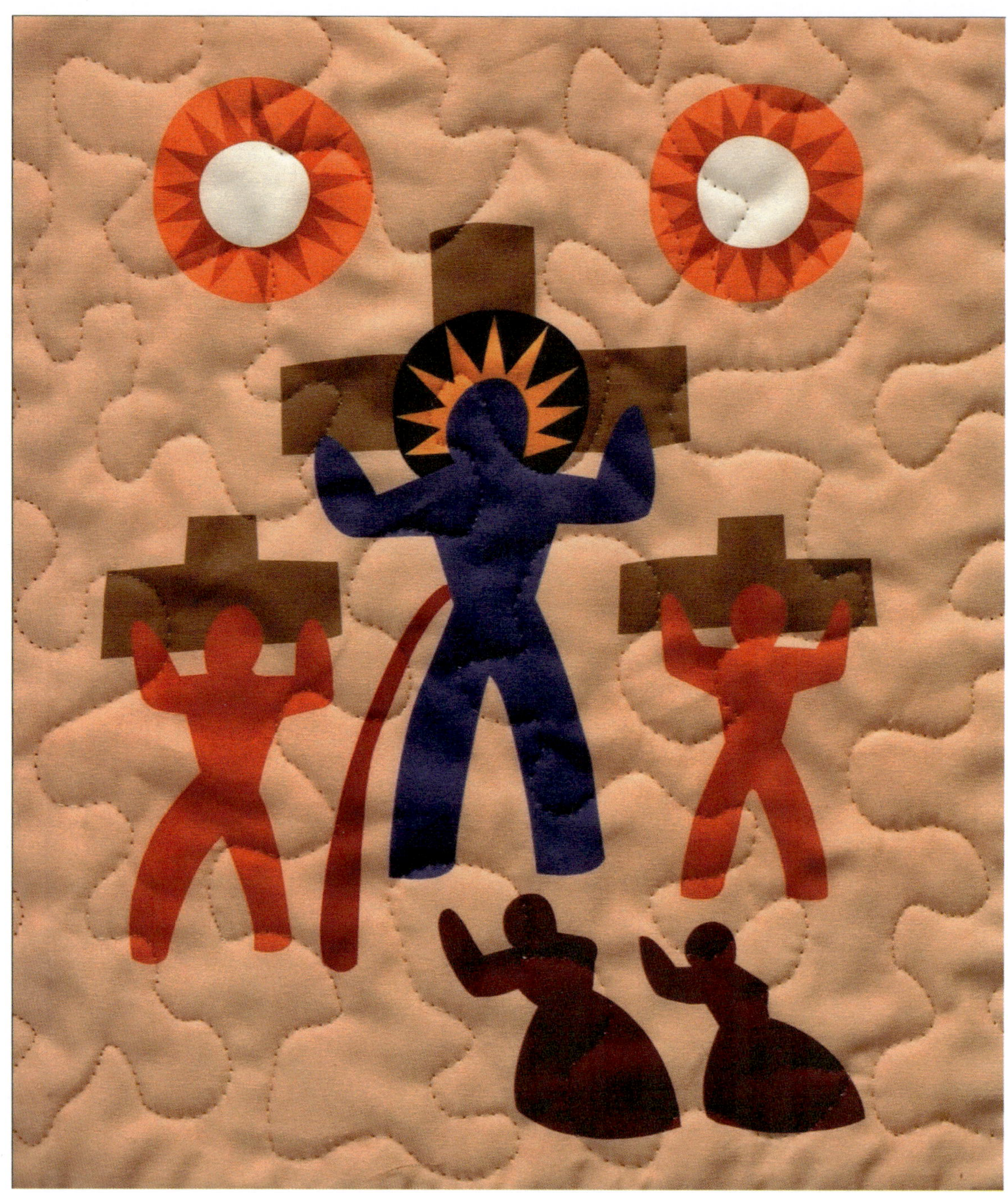

Block 11 – The Crucifixion
Luke 23: 32-34a

Two other men, both criminals, were also led out with him to be executed. When they came to the place called the Skull, there they crucified him, along with the criminals – one on his right, the other on his left. Jesus said, "Father, forgive them, for they do not know what they are doing."

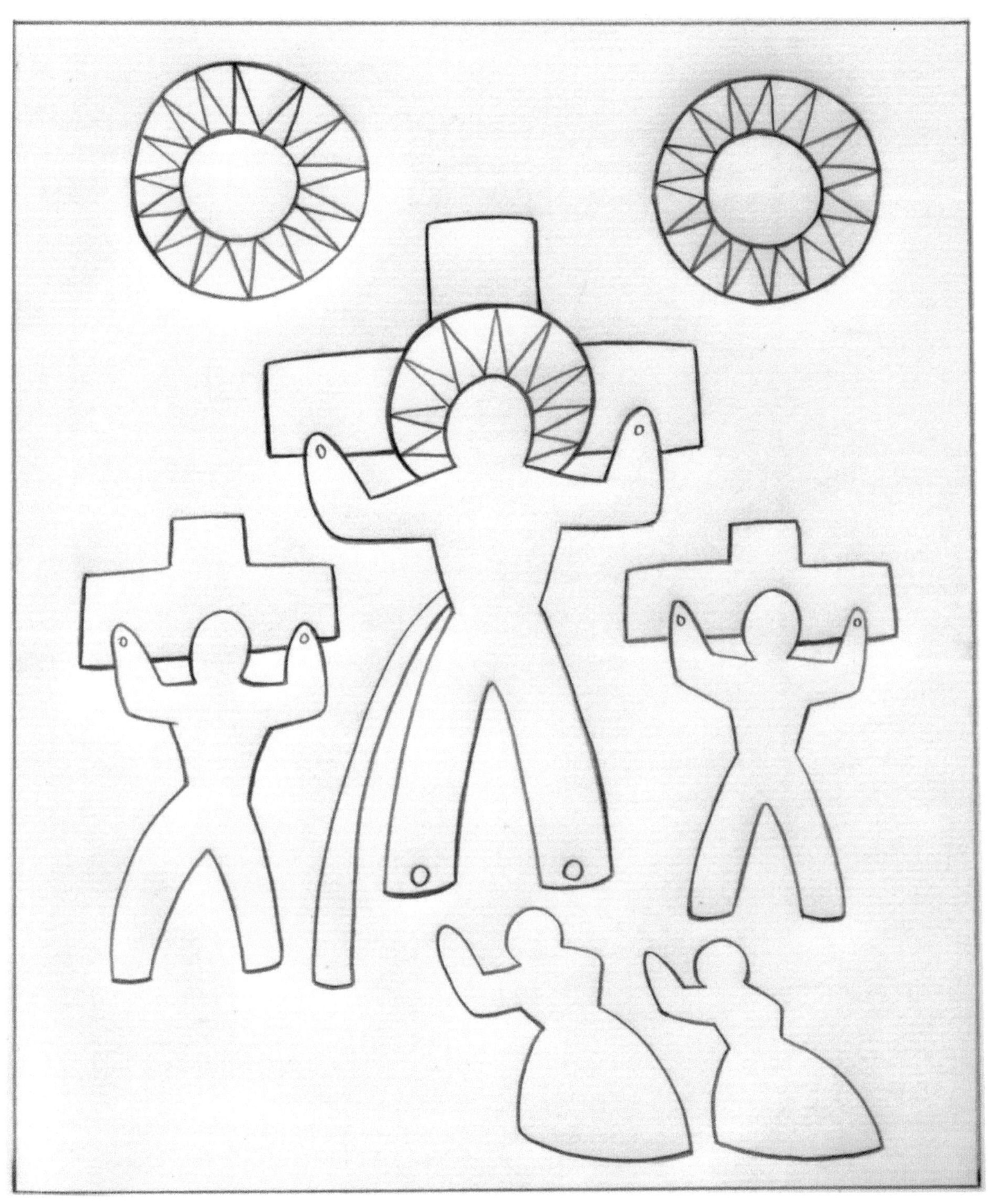

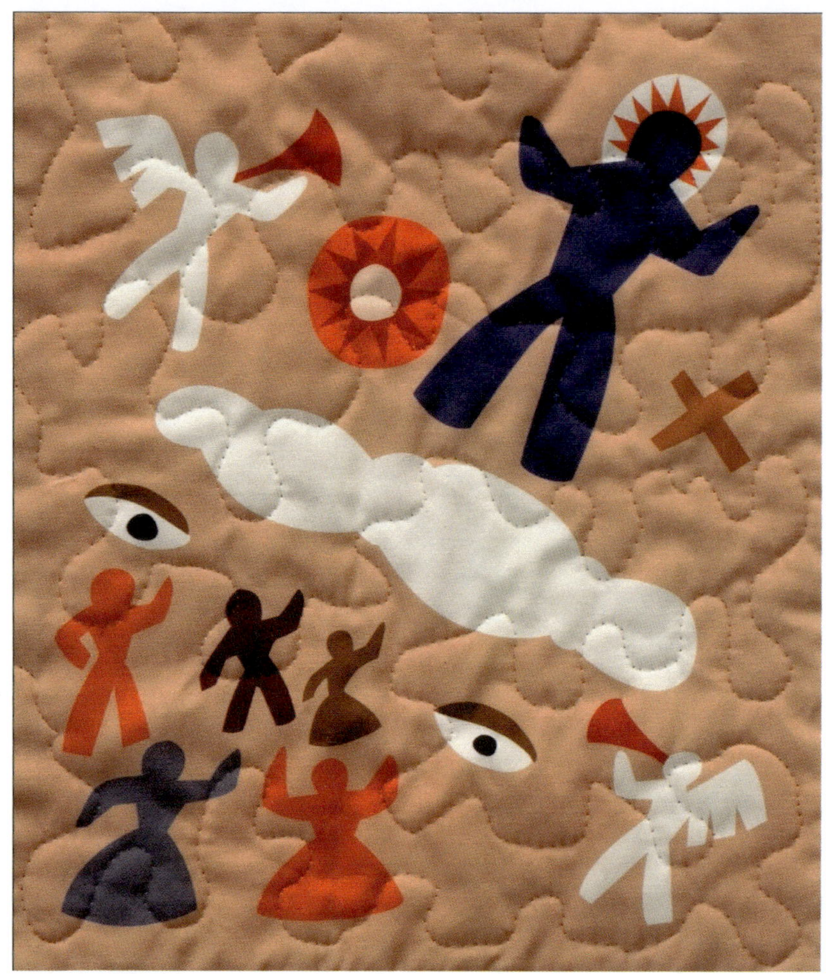

Block 12 – The Accession
Acts 1: 6 -11

So when they met together, they asked him, "Lord, are you at this time going to restore the kingdom to Israel?"

He said to them: "It is not for you to know the times or dates the Father has set by his own authority. But you will receive power when the Holy Spirit comes on you; and you will be my witnesses in Jerusalem, and in all Judea and Samaria, and to the ends of the earth.

After he said this, he was taken up before their very eyes, and a cloud hid him from their sight.

They were looking intently up into the sky as he was going, when suddenly two men dressed in white stood beside them.

"Men of Galilee," they said, "why do you stand here looking into the sky? This same Jesus, who has been taken from you into heaven, will come back in the same way you have seen him go into heaven."

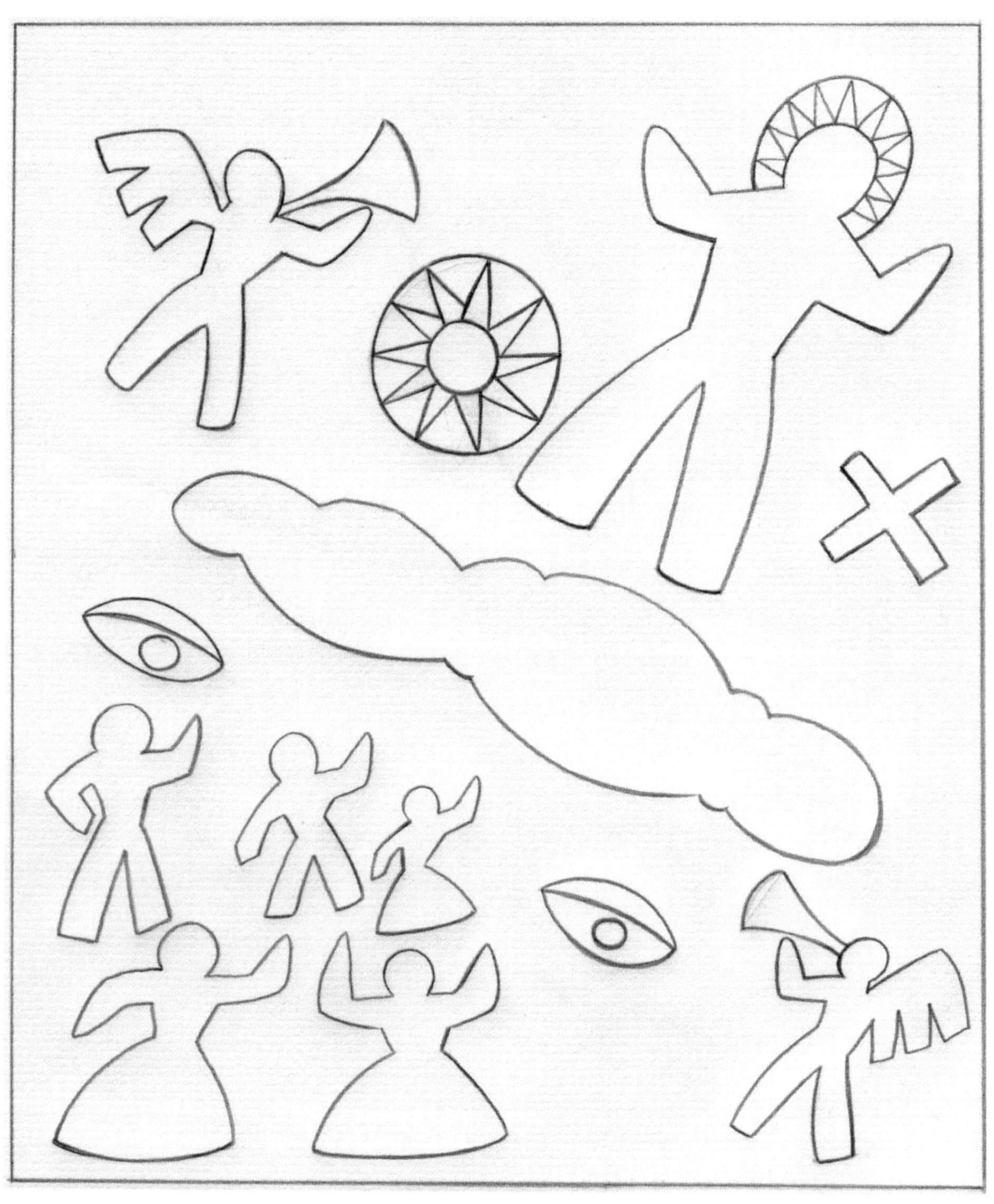

About the Author

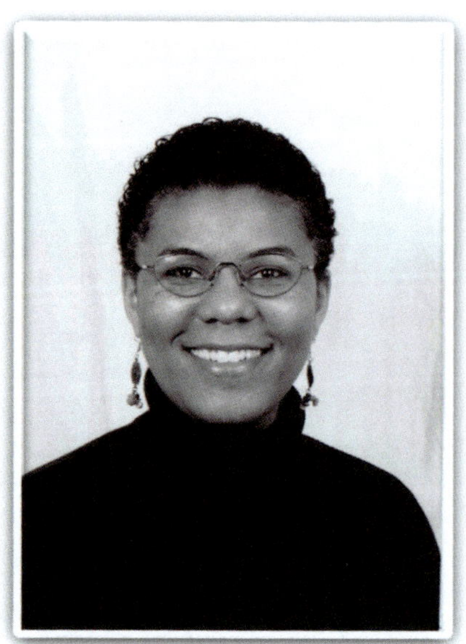

Kyra E. Hicks is a quilter. Her quilts have appeared in more than forty exhibits in the United States and abroad. Her *Black Barbie* Quilt is in the permanent collection of the Fenimore Art Museum in Cooperstown, New York as is her *Patriotic Quilt* at the Museum of Arts & Design in New York City.

Kyra loves historical, investigative research and rediscovering the lives of quilters past. She is the author of *Black Threads: An African American Quilting Sourcebook* (2003), the children's book *Martha Ann's Quilt for Queen Victoria* (2007), and *This I Accomplish: Harriet Powers' Bible Quilt and Other Pieces* (2009). Kyra hosts a blog on African American quilting news - www.BlackThreads.blogspot.com.

Kyra earned an MBA from the University of Michigan, a diploma from the London School of Economics and Political Science, and a BBA from Howard University. She lives in Arlington, Virginia, where she tends her colorful, fragrant rose garden.

Author's Note

I hope you enjoyed this book! Do feel free to drop me a note or let me know if you'd like to be on my mailing list when my next book is published. I'll give you a hint – it's also on quilting!

Kyra E. Hicks
3037 S. Buchanan Street
Arlington, VA 22206
Black.Threads@yahoo.com

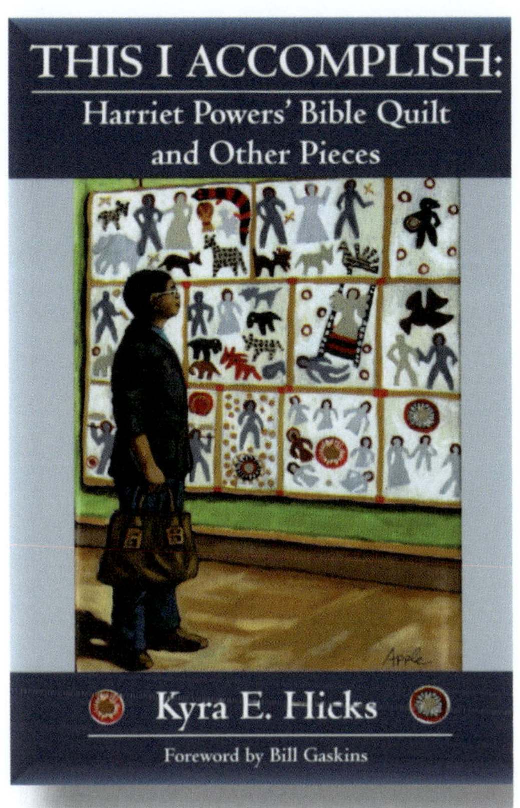

This I Accomplish: Harriet Powers' Bible Quilt and Other Pieces

The powerful quilts of Harriet Powers (1837-1910), a former Georgia slave, continue to capture our imagination today. Thousands of visitors to the Smithsonian National Museum of American History and the Museum of Fine Arts, Boston have stood transfixed viewing her *Bible Quilt* and *Pictorial Quilt*.

Until now, no one has told the entire, dramatic story of how these quilts (one sold for $5) were cherished in private homes before emerging as priceless national treasures.

"Wow! I kept leaping out of my chair!" said one reader.

Other Resources

A Pattern Book, Based on Appliqué Quilt by Mrs. Harriet Powers, American, 19th Century. Boston: Museum of Fine Arts, 1973.

Stitched From the Soul: Slave Quilts from the Ante-Bellum South by Gladys-Marie Fry. Foreword by Robert Bishop. New York: Dutton Studio Books, 1990.

"The Darling Offspring of Her Brain" by Catherine L. Homes. In *Georgia Quilts: Piecing Together A History* edited by Anita Zaleski Weinraub. Athens: University of Georgia Press, 2006.

Harriet Powers's Bible Quilts by Regenia Perry. New York: Rizzoli International Publications, Inc., 1994.

Harriett Powers Film Project, William Gilcher, Producer. Visit HarriettPowers.net.

"A Quilt Unlike Any Other": Rediscovering the Works of Harriet Powers by Laurel Thatcher Ulrich. In *Writing Women's History: A Tribute to Anne Firor Scott* edited by Elizabeth A. Payne. Jackson: University Press of Mississippi, 2011.

Printed in Dunstable, United Kingdom